Why I Still Believe...

These Are the Last Days

N.W. Hutchings
Jimmy DeYoung
Kenneth C. Hill
Ray Yerbury

Robert Lindsted
Randall Price
Mark Hitchcock
I.D.E. Thomas

All Scripture references are from the King James Version unless otherwise stated.

WHY I STILL BELIEVE THESE ARE THE LAST DAYS
Copyright © 1993 by Hearthstone Publishing, Ltd.

Printed in the United States of America

Published by:
Hearthstone Publishing, Ltd.
901 NW 6th St.
Oklahoma City, OK 73106
(405) 235-5396 ● (800) 652-1144 ● FAX (405) 236-4634

ISBN 1-879366-38-X

Table of Contents

Foreword

N.W. Hutchings

"And if I go and prepare a place for you, I will come again, and receive you unto myself; that where I am, there ye may be also" (John 14:3).

For as the lightning cometh out of the east, and shineth even unto the west; so shall also the coming of the Son of man be" (Matt. 24:27).

The angelic messengers informed the disciples on the day of Jesus' return to the Father, *"... this same Jesus, which is taken up from you into heaven, shall so come in like manner as ye have seen him go into heaven"* (Acts 1:11). In every chapter in Paul's two epistles to the church at Thessalonica the return of Jesus Christ is declared to be an irrevocable promise of God. Therefore, the question is not *if* He is coming, but rather *when* is He coming?

Now that we have established that Jesus Christ is coming back from heaven to this earth, can the time of His return be known? This is a debatable question. Jesus said of His coming again in Matthew 24:36: *"But of that day and hour knoweth no man, no, not the angels of heaven, but my Father only."*

Some who have studied the particular wording of the Greek text contend that while no date is published in the Bible for the Lord's return, it can be ascertained by investigation.

Edgar Whisenant published a controversial book entitled *Eighty-Eight Reasons Why the Rapture Will Be In 1988*. Jesus did not come in the air in 1988 to translate the Church. Mr. Whisenant explained that he was off one year in his calculations, so he published a new edition entitled *The Final Shout-- Rapture '89 Report*. The new date for the Rapture, according to Mr. Whisenant, was September 1, 1989. Once again he was in error.

There are numerical patterns in creation and in God's revelations to the prophets of Israel which indicate the end of the present age by the year A.D. 2000. However, exact date setting is arrived at by conclusion rather than by stated fact, and although there have been many date-setters for the Lord's return, all to this time have been wrong.

We do not wish to belabor the point of whether it is possible, or not possible, to determine the exact date for the Rapture or the return of Jesus Christ to establish His kingdom here on earth. What we can affirm is the certainty of knowing when His coming is near. In fact, God wants His people to know when the time of the end of the age is near. Otherwise, Jesus Christ would not have given a multitude of signs of the last days within the content of the Olivet Discourse.

In 1 Thessalonians 5:1-10, the Apostle Paul stated that the unsaved world will be oblivious to the times of the last days, but that Christians who are discerning the signs of the times can know when the day that destruction will come upon the world is near. Of the nearness of the Lord's return Paul said, *"But of the times and the seasons, brethren, ye have no need that I write unto you"* (1 Thess. 5:1). On the Hebrew calendar, a "time" was a year, and "times" was two or more years, but certainly no more than one generation. Within one year there are four seasons.

Without having to stretch the truth of God's Word, we can securely aver that according to Bible prophecy, Christians who are faithfully and accurately comparing world events to the prophetic Word can know within a few years, or even months, when the events associated with the last seven years of the present dispensation will begin to occur.

In this second volume, noted scholars of eschatology declare why they believe we are living in the last days which precede the coming of Jesus Christ.

Chapter 1

Israel—The Fig Tree
God's Number One Sign of the Last Days

N.W. Hutchings

If we were to list all the signs in the Bible identifiable with the "last days," or the "latter years," and the Second Coming of Jesus Christ, in order of importance we would have to put the return of a remnant of Israel and the refounding of the nation as number one. The following messianic signs evident in Israel today signify that the return of Jesus Christ to claim the throne of David and bring in His own government upon this earth is near; making the translation of the Church, to be followed by the Great Tribulation even nearer.

Sign No. I—The Fig Tree

From Joel, Hosea, and other prophets, Israel is declared to be God's fig tree when producing good works. But Jeremiah prophesied of Israel,

> ". . . *therefore shall they fall among them that fall: in the time of their visitation they shall be cast down, saith the Lord. I will surely consume them, saith the Lord: there shall be no grapes on the vine, nor figs on the fig tree, and the leaf shall fade; and the things that I have given*

—4—

them shall pass away from them. '' (Jer. 8:12-13)

Jesus prophesied that Jerusalem would be leveled, even to the ground, because Israel ''. . . *knewest not the time of thy visitation*'' (Luke 19:44). To literally fulfill the prophecy of Jeremiah, Jesus cursed the fig tree (Matt. 21:19-21), and leaves withered and faded away. Like the fig tree, Israel faded away as a nation, but Jesus said the fig tree would bud again as the most evident sign that His return was near. During Israel's absence from the land, all vegetation, including the fig trees, died, became sparse and scarce. Today in Israel the fig tree is growing again to heights of fifty feet and thicknesses of up to two feet. And like the fig tree, the nation is budding and putting on fruit.

> *''Now learn a parable of the fig tree; When his branch is yet tender, and putteth forth leaves, ye know that summer is nigh: So likewise ye, when ye shall see all these things, know that it* [the Son of man coming in the clouds of Heaven with power and great glory--v. 30] *is near, even at the doors''* (Matt. 24:32-33)

Sign No. 2–The Return

> *''And I will bring you out from the people, and will gather you out of the countries wherein ye are scattered, with a mighty hand, and with a stretched out arm, and with fury poured out''* (Ezek. 20:34).

There are dozens of prophecies relating to the regathering of Israel out of all nations. Jesus prophesied,

> *''And they shall fall by the edge of the sword,*

*and shall be led away captive into all nations:
and Jerusalem shall be trodden down of the
Gentiles, until the times of the Gentiles be
fulfilled. . . . And then shall they see the Son of
man coming in a cloud with power and great
glory''* (Luke 21:24,27)

Jews have returned to Israel from more than seventy
nations, and the context of prophecy is that when this occurs,
the world is to know that the coming of Messiah (return of Jesus
Christ) is at hand.

Sign No. 3—Buying Back the Land

*''Men shall buy fields for money, and sub-
scribe evidences, and seal them, and take
witnesses in the land of Benjamin, and in the
places about Jerusalem, and in the cities of
Judah, and in the cities of the mountains, and
in the cities of the valley, and in the cities of the
south: for I will cause their captivity to return,
saith the Lord''* (Jer. 32:44).

In 1903, Great Britain offered the World Zionist
Organization the country of Uganda for the establishing of a
Jewish state. The WZO rejected the offer, citing Scripture that
they must return to the land God gave Abraham. Wealthy Jews
purchased land throughout Palestine for settlement, and in
1909 the first *kibbutz* was established on the Sea of Galilee. As
prophesied, this is how the return began.

Sign No. 4—Israel Reborn In a Day

*''Who hath heard such a thing? who hath seen
such things? Shall the earth be made to bring
forth in one day? or shall a nation be born at
once? for as soon as Zion travailed, she brought*

forth her children'' (Isa. 66:8).

The rebirth of Israel as a nation in one day, May 14, 1948, was indeed the result of the travails of the World Zionist Organization in fighting both the English and the Arabs in returning the children of Abraham, Isaac, and Jacob. Israel was reborn in a day, as prophesied.

Sign No. 5—Order of Return

"For I am the Lord thy God, the Holy One of Israel, thy Saviour: I gave Egypt for thy ransom, Ethiopia and Seba for thee. Since thou wast precious in my sight, thou hast been honourable, and I have loved thee: therefore will I give men for thee, and people for thy life. Fear not: for I am with thee: I will bring thy seed from the [1] east, and gather thee from the [2] west; I will say to the [3] north, Give up; and to the [4] south, Keep not back: bring my sons from far, and my daughters from the ends of the earth; . . . Ye are my witnesses, saith the Lord, and my servant whom I have chosen: that ye may know and believe me, and understand that I am he: before me there was no God formed, neither shall there be after me. . . . This people have I formed for myself; they shall shew forth my praise. But thou hast not called upon me, O Jacob; but thou hast been weary of me, O Israel'' (Isa. 43:3-6,10,21-22).

Isaiah prophesied that though Israel would not believe, when the time for the Messiah was at hand, the Lord would regather them in their unbelief. Israel would first return from the east, and according to the *Judaic Encyclopedia*, in 1900 there were three hundred thousand Jews in Turkey; in 1939, there were only thirty thousand in Turkey. The same percentages of Jewish immigration to Israel also applied to Jordan, Syria, Iraq, Yemen, and other nations in the Middle East.

The second stage of Jewish immigration came from the west, the nations of Europe. In 1939, the Jewish population of Europe was 9,480,000; in 1948, it had dropped to 3,780,000. After the Nazi holocaust in which almost six million Jews were killed, additional thousands fled to Israel seeking a place of peace and safety.

The third phase of Jewish immigration, according to prophecy, was to come from the north. Until the *glasnost* policies of Gorbachev were initiated in Russia in 1988, the Jews were not allowed to emigrate. Then, a few began to return through Helsinki; but the prime minister of Finland closed the exit door because of Arab pressure. A constituent of our ministry, Siiki, and a friend of the prime minister's wife, informed him that unless he opened the door to Jewish emigration from Russia again, God would do to him what He did to the king of Edom. To date, over four hundred thousand Russian Jews have gone to Israel.

The fourth and final phase of the return of a remnant to prepare for the coming of Messiah would be from the south, according to Isaiah. In 1990, approximately fourteen thousand black Jews (Falasha) were flown out of Ethiopia to Israel in Operation Solomon. According to tradition, the black Jews of Ethiopia are descendants of a son born to the Queen of Sheba by Solomon (1 Kings 10). Thus, the order of the return of a Jewish remnant to await Messiah's appearance is exactly as prophesied.

Sign No. 6—A Pure Language

"Therefore wait ye upon me, saith the Lord, until the day that I rise up to the prey: for my determination is to gather the nations, that I may assemble the kingdoms, to pour upon

them mine indignation, even all my fierce anger: for all the earth shall be devoured with the fire of my jealousy. For then will I turn to the people a pure language, that they may all call upon the name of the Lord, to serve him with one consent. From beyond the rivers of Ethiopia my suppliants, even the daughter of my dispersed, shall bring mine offering'' (Zeph. 3:8-10).

In 1982, under the leadership of Eliezer Ben Yehuda, it was decided that Hebrew should be the official language of the return. As the Jews came speaking many languages and dialects, they had to go to school to learn Hebrew. Today, even the Ethiopian Jews and the Jews who have returned from Russia are going to school to learn pure Hebrew. According to the prophecy, this would take place at the time of the end, the time of Jacob's trouble and the Battle of Armageddon.

Sign No. 7—The Shekel
''And the shekel shall be twenty gerahs. . . . This is the oblation that ye shall offer. . . . All the people of the land shall give this oblation for the prince in Israel'' (Ezek. 45:12-13,16).

The shekel as the unit of monetary exchange had to be restored in order for the Israelites to give the proper offering to the Messiah at the Temple in the Millennium. In 1980, the Knesset restored the shekel as the official unit of exchange in Israel; the present value of the shekel is approximately fifty cents.

Sign No. 8—Cities of Israel
''And I will multiply upon you man and beast; and they shall increase and bring fruit: and I

will settle you after your old estates. . . . For I will take you from among the heathen, and gather you out of all countries, and will bring you into your own land" (Ezek. 36:11,24)

As the Jews return, the cities of Israel have been renamed after their old estates. Even the cities and villages associated with the ministry of Jesus bear their biblical identification: Cana, Nazareth, Jericho, Bethany, Bethlehem, etc.

Sign No. 9—Cities Exception

"Then began he to upbraid the cities wherein most of his mighty works were done, because they repented not: Woe unto thee, Chorazin! woe unto thee, Bethsaida! for if the mighty works, which were done in you, had been done in Tyre and Sidon, they would have repented long ago in sackcloth and ashes. . . . And thou, Capernaum, which art exalted unto heaven, shalt be brought down to hell: for if the mighty works, which have been done in thee, had been done in Sodom, it would have remained until this day" (Matt. 11:20-21,23).

The curses upon these three cities, in association with cities that had been destroyed in the past, indicated that they would be completely erased, never to be rebuilt again. Though the other cities of Israel have been restored and inhabited, Chorazin, Bethsaida, and Capernaum are nothing but ruins. They remain, even as the Jews return, as a testimony that Jesus Christ is the Messiah who came and that He is coming again.

Sign No. 10—From Desolation to Productivity

"Thou [Jerusalem] shalt no more be termed Forsaken; neither shall thy land any more be

termed Desolate: but thou shalt be called Hephzibah [My delight], *and thy land Beulah* [wife]: *for the Lord delighteth in thee, and thy land shall be married''* (Isa. 62:4).

"He shall cause them that come of Jacob to take root: Israel shall blossom and bud, and fill the face of the world with fruit'' (Isa. 27:6).

According to the Bible, as evidenced by history, when the Jew is absent from the land it becomes barren and desolate. When the Jew returns, the land produces its full measure. When the Jews began to return, the land was desolate and barren with no trees and very little grass. Today, the land of Israel is the most productive in the world, providing not only for the needs of the people, but vegetables, fruits, cotton, and other farming products are shipped to Europe and other nations of the world. With the exception of the coconut and the pineapple, every kind of fruit, nut, and vegetable in the world is now grown in Israel.

Sign No. 11—Irrigation

"In that day will I raise up the tabernacle of David that is fallen, and close up the breaches thereof; and I will raise up his ruins, and I will build it as in the days of old: . . . Behold, the days come, saith the Lord, that the plowman shall overtake the reaper, and the treader of grapes him that soweth seed; and the mountains shall drop sweet wine, and all the hills shall melt. . . . And I will plant them upon their land, and they shall no more be pulled up out of their land which I have given them, saith the Lord thy God'' (Amos 9:11,13,15).

Israel has developed the most efficient irrigation system in the world. As Amos prophesied, today in Israel there is crop rotation, and on one side of a field the reapers will be at work, in the middle of the field tractors will be plowing, and on the far side planters will be putting new seed in the soil. Nothing like this has ever occurred before in Israel's history, and the prophecy of Amos states that this will be a sign of the coming of Messiah to rebuild the house of David.

Sign No. 12—The Trees of Israel

"Fear not, thou worm Jacob, and ye men of Israel; I will help thee, saith the Lord, and thy redeemer, the Holy One of Israel. . . . I will plant in the wilderness the cedar, the shittah tree, and the myrtle, and the oil tree; I will set in the desert the fir tree, and the pine, and the box tree together: That they [the nations] *may see, and know, and consider, and understand together, that the hand of the Lord hath done this, and the Holy One of Israel hath created it"* (Isa. 41:14,19-20).

When Israel returned and became a nation in 1948, the mountains of Israel were completely barren. Now, trees of every kind from every nation cover these once naked hills. Southwest Radio Church planted a forest in the Valley of Elah, where David slew Goliath. God has declared when the nations of the world witness this miracle, they are to know that this is the Lord's work, and that He is ready to come again to fulfill His promises to that nation.

Sign No. 13—Vultures of Israel

"Come near, ye nations, to hear. . . . For the indignation of the Lord is upon all nations, and his fury upon all their armies. . . . Their slain also shall be cast out, and their stink shall

*come up out of their carcases. . . . For it is the
day of the Lord's vengeance, and the year of
recompences for the controversy of Zion. . . .
There shall the vultures also be gathered,
every one with her mate* " (Isa. 34:1-3,8,15).

Revelation 19:17-21 affords a graphic description of
the slain at Armageddon being consumed by the birds of Israel.
During spring and fall migration, billions of birds fly over Israel
making their way from Europe and Asia to Africa and back.
However, for the first time in centuries, vultures are again
nesting in Israel. The Israeli air force avoids vulture nesting
areas during the mating and hatching seasons. Reports have
indicated that vultures in Israel are laying two eggs now instead
of the usual one egg; but such reports are in error. Vultures in
Gamla are now actually laying four eggs at one nesting. This is
circumstantial evidence that God is increasing the bird population of Israel for the coming Battle of Armageddon.

Sign No. 14—Wild Animal Life
*"And I will rejoice in Jerusalem, and joy in my
people: and the voice of weeping shall be no
more heard in her, nor the voice of crying.
. . . The wolf and the lamb shall feed together,
and the lion shall eat straw like the bullock:
and dust shall be the serpent's meat. They shall
not hurt nor destroy in all my holy mountain,
saith the Lord"* (Isa. 65:19,25).

While the preceding messianic prophecy looks forward
to the Millennium, even today as the forest and ecology of
Israel are restored, wild animals that inhabited the land in Bible
times are returning. Ibex (biblical wild goats) gather in herds at
watering holes, coneys are increasing in number, and signs at
En-gedi warn of leopards.

Sign No. 15—Increasing Rainfall

"Blow ye the trumpet in Zion, and sound an alarm in my holy mountain: let all the inhabitants of the land tremble: for the day of the Lord cometh, for it is nigh at hand; ... Be glad then, ye children of Zion, and rejoice in the Lord your God: for he hath given you the former rain moderately, and he will cause to come down for you the rain, the former rain, and the latter rain in the first month" (Joel 2:1,23).

In Bible times, there were two seasons of rain in Israel-- the spring and fall. During the Diaspora, the fall rains ceased; but as Joel prophesied, with Israel's return, the latter rains have returned also. The average rainfall between 1931 and 1960 in Israel was 21.1 inches. But in 1980, the average rainfall in Israel had increased to 29.1 inches, almost 40 percent. The percentage of rainfall increase has matched the increase in the Jewish population of Israel. Ninety percent of water used in Israel comes from the Sea of Galilee. Jerusalem usually gets a brief dusting of snow every three or four years. This past winter, Jerusalem received four blizzards with snow depths ranging from one to two feet. Yehuda Levy, publisher of the *Jerusalem Post*, reported to us that nothing like this had ever happened in the history of Israel. The Sea of Galilee is overflowing in spite of increased water usage. Joel prophesied that the restoration of the latter rains to Israel would be a sign to the world of coming catastrophic events to conclude with the coming of the Lord to dwell in Zion.

Sign No. 16—Jerusalem, An International Problem

"Behold, I will make Jerusalem a cup of trembling unto all the people round about, when they shall be in the siege both against

Judah and against Jerusalem'' (Zech. 12:2).

Since 1967, East Jerusalem, the biblical Jerusalem where the Temple is located, has been a subject of controversy to all members of the United Nations. The Arabs classified East Jerusalem as occupied territory, but Israel contends that there is only one Jerusalem--and it belongs to Israel. Israel names Jerusalem its capital, yet the United Nations refuses to recognize it as the capital city of Israel. As Zechariah prophesied, Jerusalem is a problem to all nations, a sign that Israel will soon recognize the Messiah at His coming by the nail prints in His hands (vs. 10).

Sign No. 17—A Democracy

*''And the governors of Judah shall say in
their heart, The inhabitants of Jerusalem
shall be my strength in the Lord of hosts
their God''* (Zech. 12:5).

Zechariah prophesied that Israel in the last days would be ruled not by a king or prince, but by governors. This statement by the prophet implies not a kingdom, not a dictatorship, not a theocracy, but a democracy. Israel was indeed refounded as a democracy; in fact, the only true democracy in the entire Middle East.

Sign No. 18—Wars of Israel and Jerusalem Retaken

*''In that day will I make the governors of Judah
like an hearth of fire among the wood, and like
a torch of fire in a sheaf; and they shall devour
all the people round about, on the right hand
and on the left . . .''* (Zech. 12:6).

The overwhelming victories of tiny Israel over vastly superior armies of Egypt (on the left hand) and Syria and Jordan (on the right hand), in 1948, 1967, and 1973, amazed the entire world. Zechariah in this prophecy is not referring to Armageddon, because only Israel is involved. At Armageddon, Israel will be hiding in a place of refuge. This prophecy can refer only to the recent victories of Israel, a prelude, according to Zechariah, of the coming of Messiah to stand upon the Mount of Olives (Zech. 12:4) "... *And Jerusalem shall be inhabited again in her own place, even in Jerusalem*" (Zech. 12:6). Zechariah prophesied that in one of the wars in which Israel would be victorious, Jerusalem would be inhabited again, in its own place. After the establishing of Israel as a nation in 1948, there were two Jerusalems--the new city occupied by the Jews, and the old city where the Temple site is, is occupied by the Arabs. At the amazing 1967 Six-Day War, Israel occupied the old city of Jerusalem, and Jerusalem was inhabited again in its own rightful place.

Sign No. 19—The Diaspora

"For the children of Israel shall abide many days without a king, and without a prince, and without a sacrifice. . . . Afterward shall the children of Israel return. . . . Hear the word of the Lord. . . . I will go and return to my place, till they acknowledge their offence, and seek my face: in their affliction they will seek me early. Come, and let us return unto the Lord: for he hath torn, and he will heal us; he hath smitten, and he will bind us up. After two days will he revive us: in the third day he will raise us up, and we shall live in his sight" (Hos. 3:4-5; 4:1; 5:15; 6:1-2).

As prophesied by Hosea, Israel was dispersed for many days without a nation, a government, or a place of worship. After two days, according to the prophecy, God would restore them to favor, and in the third day, glorify the nation and revive His people. One day counts as a thousand years with God (Ps. 90:4; 2 Pet. 3:8), and the dispersion of Israel lasted for approximately two thousand years. As indicated in *The Rise and Fall of the Roman Empire* by Gibbons, the early Church fathers taught that the Lord would return in two thousand years. As the calendar looks forward to the year 2000 (the third day), Israel lives in expectation of the messianic age.

Sign No. 20—Restoration of Temple Worship
"When ye therefore shall see the abomination of desolation, spoken of by Daniel the prophet, stand in the holy place, (whoso readeth, let him understand:) Then let them which be in Judaea flee into the mountains" (Matt. 24:15-16).

The Abomination of Desolation, referred to three times by Daniel and by the Apostle Paul in 2 Thessalonians 2:4, entails the stopping of Temple worship by the Antichrist, meaning that Temple worship must first be restored. Orthodox Jews by the thousands pray at the Western Wall every day for the rebuilding of the Temple. A *yeshiva* adjacent to the Temple site is fashioning vessels and instruments used in sacrificial worship. Priests clothing is also woven according to biblical instructions. These preparations for the resumption of Jewish sacrificial worship are a sure sign that the Day of the Lord is very near.

Yasser Arafat, after signing the peace agreement with Prime Minister Rabin of Israel in Washington, D.C. on September 13, was asked on a national television program how he would reconcile his claim to old Jerusalem when Israel still claimed it as the national capital. Arafat replied that the major area of contention with Israel was the Holy Place and that matter could be resolved later. In Arafat's statement, the possibility of the PLO organization's granting Israel the right to rebuild the Temple on Mount Moriah in exchange for relinquishing other rights to the city comes into view.

Sign No. 21—Comprehensive Middle East Peace Treaty

"And he shall confirm the covenant with many for one week: and in the midst of the week he shall cause the sacrifice and the oblation to cease . . . " (Dan. 9:27).

A week on the Jewish calendar could be seven days, seven years, seven thousand years, etc. (Gen. 29:27-28). From the context of Daniel 9, it is evident that the covenant will be seven years, and "he" means the Antichrist, because this deceitful act introduces the "time of Jacob's trouble." The "covenant" refers to the everlasting covenant God made with Abraham, giving the patriarch's seed the right to the land his feet would pass over (Gen. 12:1-4). There must be a comprehensive peace treaty between Israel and the unilateral authority that will guarantee Israel's right to the land and include an agreement where the Jews may resume Temple worship.

While the agreement signed between the government of Israel and the Palestinian Liberation Organization on September 13 is not the covenant of Daniel 9:27 which will begin the Tribulation, most Mideast political observers believe a more comprehensive peace treaty will be signed by the end of 1994.

Sign No. 22—The Sealed Gate

"Then he brought me back the way of the gate of the outward sanctuary which looketh toward the east; and it was shut. Then said the Lord unto me; This gate shall be shut, it shall not be opened, and no man shall enter in by it; because the Lord, the God of Israel, hath

*entered in by it, therefore it shall be shut. It is
for the prince; the prince, he shall sit in it to eat
bread before the Lord; he shall enter by the
way of the porch of that gate, and shall go out
by the way of the same* " (Ezek. 44:1-3).

The gate of the outward sanctuary, the Eastern Gate,
was the gate by which Jesus entered when He stayed in
Bethany, came over the Mount of Olives, and went into the
Temple area. According to the prophecy, this gate is to be shut
until the Prince of Israel, the Messiah, comes. This gate was
sealed shut when the walls were rebuilt by the Turks in the
sixteenth century. Arab guards are stationed at the Eastern
Gate today to keep anyone from trying to open it. According
to Ezekiel, the gate will not be opened until the Messiah comes.

Sign No. 23—Remnant of Edom

" *. . . I raise up the tabernacle of David that is
fallen, and close up the breaches thereof; and
I will raise up his ruins, and I will build it as in
the days of old: That they may possess the
remnant of Edom . . .* " (Amos 9:11-12).

Where is the remnant of Edom, the last descendants of
Esau, today? When Judah was weak as a result of the Babylonian
captivity, the Edomites moved out of Petra en masse into Israel,
and the Nabateans (descendants of Ishmael) moved up from
Arabia into Edom. The Edomites never left Israel. The Herods
were Edomites. The remnant of Esau today are the Palestinian
Arabs, and the controversy between the descendants of Jacob
and the descendants of Esau indicates the time for the raising
up of the Tabernacle of David is near.

Sign No. 24—Jewish Unbelief

" *. . . blindness in part is happened to Israel,*

until the fulness of the Gentiles be come in'' (Rom. 11:25).

According to Zechariah 12:10; Matthew 23:39; Acts 15:13-17; 28:26-28; Romans 25; and Revelation 1:7, Israel, except a relatively small number, will not believe that Jesus Christ is their Messiah until they see the nail prints in His hands. If the Jewish nation today was converted to faith in Jesus Christ as the Messiah, then the Bible would not be true. In spite of the mighty witness evident to Israel today that Jesus Christ is the promised Redeemer (Isa. 28:10-12), their continued unbelief is a sign in itself of the nearness of the Lord's second coming.

Huge signs near the Temple Mount hail the soon coming of Messiah, but the Messiah that observing Jews today are looking for is not Jesus. We know according to the prophecies that Israel will accept a false messiah, the Antichrist.

Sign No. 25—Church Unbelief

''Knowing this first, that there shall come in the last days scoffers, walking after their own lusts, And saying, Where is the promise of his coming? . . . For this they willingly are ignorant of . . .'' (2 Pet. 3:3-5).

The greatest promise given in the Bible related to the return of Jesus Christ is the budding of the fig tree: the return of Israel to the land to precede the rebuilding of the Tabernacle of David. The rejection of messianic signs in Israel by the vast majority of ministers and pastors is a sign, according to Peter, that the second coming of Jesus Christ, the Day of the Lord, in which He will come as a thief in the night, is at hand.

Surely it is time for Christians to begin looking up, for the Rapture, the day of translation from this earth to heavenly places, must be on God's immediate timetable.

Chapter 2

Peace Treaty: True or False?

Jimmy DeYoung

As if he were looking around to see if anyone was eavesdropping on our conversation, the hushed voice on the other end of the telephone line whispered the question to me: ''Have we just seen the State of Israel sign a peace treaty with the Antichrist?'' Before I could answer, my mind was flooded with thoughts of what I had just witnessed. I had to agree the events of the last several hours could well have been one of the greatest events in history. From my vantage point, in front of a wide-screen television in the Government Press Office in Jerusalem, I had been an eye-witness to this event that almost took my breath away. Internationally, there was an audience that was going through many of the same emotional swings that I was going through. This was affirmed by the comments of the many foreign journalists who joined me as we sat with our eyes fixed on the screen.

Then the double doors on the White House swung open and out stepped the President of the United States, Bill Clinton, and his two honored guests. This trio made their way onto and across the White House lawn to the podium that was center stage for the three thousand or so assembled, invited guests. United States senators, ambassadors of many countries, Arab and Jewish businessmen, heads of state from various countries, and former U.S. presidents and secretaries of state were sprinkled throughout this "very important people" congregation. The television cameras that would telecast this ceremony internationally, would catch a glimpse of two notebooks containing some very important papers, laying atop a historic wooden table, the one used at the signing of the Camp David Accords.

The trio, led by President Clinton, arrived to tremendous applause and the proceedings would continue with speeches, signing of documents, and handshakes that would punctuate this ceremony as a history making event. The most significant aspect of this ceremony was the signing of a peace treaty, or a Declaration of Principle, as it's been referred to. The trio member to the right side of the U.S. president, the leader of the Jewish state of Israel, Prime Minister Yitzhak Rabin, would delegate his foreign minister, Shimon Peres, to sign this historic document. The remaining trio member, the one to Bill Clinton's left, Chairman Yasser Arafat, would delegate a senior PLO official, Mahmoud Abbas, to place his signature on this agreement that would provide for self-rule in the territories, beginning with Gaza and Jericho. The signators would also countersign the letters of recognition which Rabin and Arafat had signed only one week earlier.

With two old enemies pledging themselves to trying to forge a peaceful tomorrow, it sounded like the Middle East's past would no longer have to bury its future. Prime Minister Yitzhak Rabin's stirring speech captured the gravity of the occasion. Rabin, known for his lack of eloquence, seized the emotional center of the day in possibly one of his best speeches. He spoke not in euphoric terms, but rather of *"hope mixed with apprehension."* Rabin spoke briefly, simply, and at times even poetically, with a magnanimity of spirit. While displaying sensitivity to those who had suffered in the past, he spoke movingly of the potential for the future.

Putting the event in human terms, he spelled out the context of the ceremony: the hope for an end to bitter conflict rather than for total harmony. After reading the famous, ''To everything there is a season'' section from Ecclesiastes, he concluded, *''The time has come for peace.''*

Rabin also reached out to the Palestinian, *''Enough of blood and tears. Enough. . . . We are today giving peace a chance and saying to you: Enough. Let us pray that a day will come when we all will say: Farewell to arms.''*

As I sat there in the Government Press Office, with Rabin's words echoing through my mind, there was joy and sadness. There was relief and bitterness. There was hope and despair. But then I was flooded with thoughts that seemed to divide themselves into three categories: the geo-political, the biblical, and the prophetic. Intertwined with information, knowledge, and a predetermined mindset, I decided I needed to get alone and separate my thinking into the proper departments.

Arriving at my apartment, I faced the task of thinking through all that I had witnessed. With my understanding of the biblical background and prophetic scripture, I was confronted with the phone call seeking my opinion as an analyst of the occurrence at the White House. Was this the peace treaty spoken of in Scripture, and was Arafat the Antichrist? Before I answer that question, allow me to share how I thought through this whole situation.

Geo-Political

First, an analysis from the strictly geo-political side. In the typical Israeli there is mixed emotion as well--he is so eager for peace, an end to death and destruction in his homeland. There is not one family in the state of Israel that hasn't been touched by either the death of war or the devastation of a terrorist attack. There hasn't been a year, in fact there hasn't been a month, since Israel became a nation in 1948 that there hasn't been some Jewish son or daughter that's been killed in war or murdered in cold blood by a terrorist. That kind of everyday, every-family situation causes all Israelis to grasp at anything or anyone that promises peace. But at the same time, they wonder if this agreement between the Rabin-led Israeli government and Yasser Arafat and his PLO, is truly the real peace treaty they look for, or does it have problems?

It is not necessary to believe in the accuracy of opinion polls to realize that a majority of Israelis and Palestinians support the Israel-PLO agreement. In the beginning, jubilation and euphoria was everywhere. The prospect of peace, especially after scores of years of bloodshed and war, is welcomed with ecstasy. It's almost indecent to suggest that the euphoria may be unwarranted. Yet it is difficult to escape the nagging suspicion that the September celebration on the White House lawn was, at best, premature. From a strictly geo-political point of view there are problems that lay heavy over this whole process.

The most glaring problem is the inception of the agreement. This accord, that was signed on the White House lawn, came out of the series of secret, in fact denied meetings between representatives of each party. The Rabin government cited as the reason for negotiations in total secrecy, the fact that only undisclosed talks could bring results. Maintaining total secrecy in today's leaky world is not easy. The Israeli government must be congratulated for keeping the talks hermetically sealed for so long. But the price of its success has not been negligible. First and foremost, the government has lost credibility. It did not only falsely deny it had contacts with the PLO throughout the secret negotiations, it actually spoke against the advisability of such contacts.

To make matters worse, it was the PLO—whose reputation for fabrication and disinformation used to be second to none--which told the truth when it insisted that talks at a high level were taking place, while Israel was lying. This puts in doubt governmental denials of PLO claims regarding the interpretation of the current Gaza/Jericho agreement.

The second problem with secret talks is that many who should have been consulted were kept out of the loop. One of those out of the loop was deputy chief of staff Maj. Gen. Amanon Shahad, who is responsible for security of Israel. The general told the Knesset Foreign Affairs and Defense Committee that he doubts the army can provide the protection for Israelis, which the agreement stipulates. Even more serious is the crippling effect the agreement will have on the war against terrorism which will still be very present in the territories.

Perhaps the most bothersome aspect of the agreement, particularly for those concerned about the human rights of the Palestinian Arabs, is the license the PLO will have to bring order to the Gaza and Jericho districts. The PLO will not act under the constraints applied to the Israeli Defense Force. This means the new Palestinian police--which PLO sources say will number between fifteen and thirty thousand--will act the way all security forces in dictatorial Arab countries act: with unbounded brutality and total disregard for international norms. Arafat's regime, both in Jordan and Lebanon, was an unspeakably cruel, totalitarian dictatorship. Arafat's *Fatah*, after all, has been more active than any other organization in the torture-murder of collaborators in the territories. They will now be able to get rid of their opponents with full Israeli approval.

Any analysis of the ceremony at the White House would cause concerns about those ingredients that may have gone unnoticed by most observers. As the trio of Bill Clinton, Yitzhak Rabin, and Yasser Arafat emerged from the White House, it was striking to note that all participants had on dress suits. But one principal, Chairman Arafat, had on a dress military outfit. One commentator brought out the fact that Arafat was saying by his attire that if he couldn't accomplish his goals through diplomatic means then he would revert to his normal ''*modus operandi*,'' the militant route.

Listening to the speeches was revealing to those who were looking for signals. The Arabic speeches by PLO leaders

Yasser Arafat and Mahmoud Abbas may have signaled PLO intentions in ways that went undetected by most English and Hebrew speakers, but not by the PLO's primary Arabic-speaking audience.

The speeches were important not only for what they said and how they said it, but for what they didn't say. Arafat spoke of returning to "our country"--using the term *bilaadina*, which has a very charged meaning for every Palestinian leader. The Palestinian national anthem is called "Balaadi, Balaadi" ("My Country, My Country") and is often sung as a protest song at demonstrations. Both Arafat and Abbas--each of whom speak English--preferred to speak Arabic, not only because it is their mother tongue, but also because it allowed them to use language which serves as code words for their followers.

Aiming their remarks primarily at the Arabic-speaking audiences, their most salient messages were continued devotion to the right of return of refugees from all wars with Israel; determination to establish a Palestinian state; and refusal to accept the legitimacy of Zionism.

Both Arafat and Abbas used the term *marahil*--"stages" in Arabic--conjuring up in the Arab audience's mind the image of the two men's continued devotion to "The Strategy of Stages," the PLO doctrine adopted in 1974 for using a diplomatic settlement to obtain a base for the continued struggle against Israel.

It is interesting to note the comments of Amos Oz, an Israeli novelist famous for his intense sympathy for the Palestinian Arabs. He told a Los Angeles audience:

> *"To my regret I have learned over the years that the statements they make in Arabic are a thousand times more important than what they are likely to whisper in the ears of people who are eager for peace."*

Blatantly absent from Arafat's speech, either in Arabic or English, was his promised statement renouncing terrorism and violence. On September 9, 1993, Arafat sent a letter to the Norwegian foreign minister, Johan Jergen Holst, with a copy to Prime Minister Rabin, that he would make a public statement calling upon the Palestinian people to take part in the steps leading to the normalization of life, rejecting violence and terrorism, and contributing to peace and stability in the region. In fact, he would have had a perfect opportunity to fulfill his promise while speaking at the White House, especially in light of the two terrorist attacks on Israelis in Israel the day before the historic event in Washington.

This leads to one final thought in the geo-political area before we look at the biblical aspect of this analysis. The biggest concern anyone should have has gone unspoken, especially at the White House ceremonies. That concern is the trustworthiness of Yasser Arafat. There is no other person in the history of this world with more Jewish blood on his hands than Arafat, except Adolph Hitler. The litany of brutal terrorist acts ordered by Arafat would include Jewish athletes at the Olympics in Munich, United States citizens on foreign soil, and many others too numerous to discuss now. In addition to the aforementioned, you must add to the list over one thousand Palestinians that have been murdered, at the orders of Yasser Arafat, because they were collaborating with Israel.

Not only has Arafat ordered the murders of many innocent people, but in the process he has lied about his true intentions. You might recall that in December of 1988 he renounced terrorism and then proceeded to direct the *intifada* that has lasted for these last five years. It's hard to understand how Israel would allow itself to sit and negotiate, much less sign an agreement with, a murdering liar.

Many Israeli's who are opposed to the agreement have compared Prime Minister Yitzhak Rabin to the late British Prime Minister Neville Chamberlain, who took the word of

Hitler and announced to Britain everything was okay. Chamberlain, as he lay dying, in December 1940, at the height of the German bombing blitz, exclaimed, *"Everything would have been all right if Hitler hadn't lied to me."* Only time will tell now how close the comparison will be.

Biblical

The application of biblical truth to this situation will give the reader much insight which will lead to understanding and consolation in such a time as this. Before we shed the light of God's Word on the subject it will benefit us to look at some principles of Islamic thought.

The absence of peace in the Middle East, and in particular in the portion that has been inhabited by the Jewish people, is due to the occupation of a piece of land. You must keep in mind that the whole conflict is over land. Moslems believe that the land in question (present-day Israel) was once given to the Jewish people by God, but because of disobedience the land was forfeited. As a result the Jews suffered expulsion, and God then gave the kingdom promises to those more worthy and faithful--the descendants of Ishmael and their representatives, the Moslems.

Since all people who are not of the Islamic faith are considered unbelievers, to the Moslem the state of Israel represents the defeat of believers by unbelievers, the humiliation of righteous Islam by the "evil Jews." This makes the call for *jihad* (holy war) a must. It is essential for the Jewish people to return to the submissive, menial role God has decreed for them, which does not include possession of the holy land of Palestine.

A Jewish presence in the Middle East causes the modern Moslem to wrestle with the variance between their theology and their experiences. Technological advances, victory after victory in military conflicts, and various other apparent successes cause the Moslem fundamentalist to conclude that they must retake the Holy Land for Islam and, by so doing, re-establish and reconfirm Islamic superiority over the discredited faith of the Jews.

As in the days of Saladin, who drove out the Crusaders in A.D. 1187, the Moslems are concerned that, by allowing the Jewish people to "take over Palestine," Islamic holy sites are in danger of being subjugated in other countries as well as Israel.

One final reason for a potential Islamic holy war is the Moslem law which states there are only two realms of habitation in the world: those places that are under Islamic authority (called the "house of Islam") and those that are not. Once a piece of land becomes a part of the "house of Islam," it is considered Islamic territory forever, regardless of who dominates it or for how long.

> *"The land of Palestine (modern-day Israel) is an 'Islamic waqf' (holy possession) consecrated for future Moslem generations until judgment day. No one can renounce it or any part of it, or abandon it or any part of it."*

This statement is from the covenant of the militant Islamic fundamentalist group, known as *Hamas*. This group, operating within the borders of Israel, believes that any Islamic territory that is not under Moslem sovereignty must be regained. This thought is instilled in the hearts of observant Moslems from an early age. Thus, it is incumbent upon fundamentalist Moslems to institute a holy war against Israel, because they occupy and rule over "Moslem land."

President Assad of Syria made a statement recently that sheds further light on this subject. He said:

> *"The reason for the conflict in the Middle East is that Israel believes the Bible. The Jews*

believe the Bible gives them all this land.''

In the search for the title deed to the land of Israel, therefore, we should be careful to look in the proper place of registration; that is, the revealed Word of God.

The question of who the land belongs to can only be answered by investigating God's Word. God is still in charge and has stated who the land belongs to, and in fact, who has possession of the whole earth. Psalm 24:1 says, *''the earth is the Lord's and the fullness thereof.''* In the book of the law, Leviticus, God gives instructions to the Jewish people about the land where they were then living. In the first twenty-two verses of Leviticus 25, God gives the Israelites His directive about the Sabbath (seventh year) for the land and the law for the Year of Jubilee (the fiftieth year) for the land. Then in the twenty-third verse God lets the Jew, the Moslem, the Christian, in fact everyone know who the land in question really belongs to: it belongs to God, Himself. He says, *''for the land is mine.''* He then tells the Jewish people that they are strangers and sojourners in the land. In other words, they are to be the caretakers of His land.

God had appeared personally to Abraham and made a promise that all the land he could see (Gen. 13:14-18), *''to thee will I give it, and to thy seed for ever.''* The word ''ever'' is the Hebrew word *owlam*, which means forever, everlasting, perpetual, and eternal. It is the same word used in Genesis 21:33 to describe the eternality of God, when it refers to Him as ''The everlasting God.''

According to Genesis 17:17-21, God made an unconditional covenant with Abraham and his son Isaac, and his grandson Jacob and all their descendants. That covenant, the Abrahamic covenant, is described in Genesis 13:7-17. A further study of this portion of Scripture will indicate that Abraham had no part in the covenant; God caused a deep sleep to come upon Abraham. Whereas two were to make the covenant—across between the two pieces of the slaughtered animals—only one, God, made the past between the divided animals, revealing His statement that the keeping of the covenant was only dependent upon Him, not Abraham.

God, who made the covenant with Abraham, then states that, *"Unto thy seed have I given this land, from the river of Egypt unto the great river, the river Euphrates"* (Gen. 15:18). The covenant plainly describes the land spoken of for Israeli possession. There are many portions of scripture that discuss Israel's true biblical borders, but time and space will not allow us to thoroughly discuss those borders. But from that expanded study one could conclude that the land God promised Abraham and his descendants is ten times what Israel has in their control today. It would include either a portion or all of the nations of Egypt, Lebanon, Syria, Iraq, Saudi Arabia, and Jordan. Of course, it would include all of what is modern-day Israel, which means Gaza and Jericho.

God has given the Jews this land. A further study of the prophecies about the land seems to indicate that the complete fulfillment of these promises will take place in the future time referred to as the "Millennial Kingdom." Ezekiel 36 refers to the land at least thirty-five times. God's promise to Abraham must be kept. God must give Abraham's descendants the land. Verse 22 says that God will do this, not for the sake of Israel, but for His holy name's sake. Hebrews 6:13 says that, *"when God made promise to Abraham, because he could swear no greater, he sware by himself."* For His holy name's sake He will give all the land promised to Abraham and his descendants.

Regarding the Islamic claim that the covenant has been transferred to the descendants of Ishmael, again the Word of God speaks for itself. In Genesis 17:18 Abraham pleaded with God to make Ishmael the recipient of the covenant. God not only denied Abraham's request, but He specifically identified Isaac as the line through which the promise would come (Gen. 17:19). Yes, the Lord would bless Ishmael too (Gen. 17:20).

"But my covenant will I establish with Isaac" (Gen. 17:21).

Christians must understand that underlying the political turmoil of the Middle East is a religious dispute. Throughout this region there is a spiritual battle being waged. Being true to God's Word should cause Christians to be hesitant to take a position that undermines Israel's right to the land God gave them. Otherwise, they may find themselves fighting against God (Acts 5:39).

Prophetic

The Bible also speaks of a peace on the earth. Isaiah 2:1-4 describes a time when the Temple will be standing on the Temple Mount in Jerusalem. All the nations of the world will go up to the Temple to have Him teach them His ways. The nations will beat their swords into plowshares and their spears into pruninghooks. The nations will not lift up their swords against each other, in fact, neither will they learn of war any more. Isaiah 11:6-9 relates that it will be so peaceful during that time that fierce enemies in the animal world will dwell together in harmony and even the little child that is leading them will play with the poisonous snake.

This peace is to reign on the earth when the Prince of Peace, Jesus Christ, the Messiah, is ruling and reigning from His throne in the Temple in Jerusalem. This period of peace is known as the Millennial Kingdom. It is a thousand-year period that is in the future. This Kingdom period, when once again a theocracy will be established on the earth, has been promised to the Jewish people for almost four thousand years.

The Jewish people long for this period of promised peace. But prior to the period of peace on earth perilous times are forecast. The Bible is very specific about the period of persecution that will precede the peace. In Jeremiah 30, the prophet refers to this terrible time as the "time of Jacob's trouble."

When Christ revealed to Daniel the pre-written history

of the Jewish people for four hundred and ninety years (the seventy weeks of Daniel), He concluded with a description of the last seven years of these four hundred and ninety. This seventieth week of Daniel is significant in light of the present peace accord between Israel and the PLO. We'll discuss it more in a moment.

A description of the seven years referred to in the New Testament as the Tribulation period can be found in Revelation 4-19. The Tribulation period has a threefold purpose: to bring to conclusion the time of the Gentiles; to bring to defeat the satanic trinity--Satan, the Antichrist, and the False Prophet; and to turn the Jewish people to their Messiah, the Lord Jesus Christ. God will use this perilous period of persecution to accomplish His goals. But in so doing, there will be much trouble on this earth.

During the seven-year Tribulation period there will be three sets of seven judgments that will get progressively worse. These twenty-one judgments will be used of God to accomplish His purpose for the Tribulation. The first of these twenty-one judgments will be the introduction to the world of a powerful personality. This individual, known as the Little Horn, the Prince that shall come, or best known as the Antichrist will spring to power and prominence at the beginning of the seven-year Tribulation period.

Daniel 9:27 recites the scenario of this one-world ruler, the Antichrist. In fact, the beginning of the seven years of persecution is marked by the confirmation of a peace treaty (false though it will be) imposed on the Jewish people. The answer to the question of whether this present agreement between Israel and the PLO is this foretold ''peace treaty,'' is obvious when a study is done of Daniel 9:27. The answer is an unequivocal ''no,'' this is not the prophesied peace agreement.

Though this present agreement is not the prophesied peace treaty, there are some very thought provoking similarities. The coming peace treaty will be ''confirmed with many.''

This language seems to indicate that not all the Jews will be in favor of the treaty of Daniel 9:27. This treaty will be imposed upon the Jews. This same type of imposition has been the procedure with the Israeli/PLO Declaration of Principles. As mentioned, the present accord was conceived in secrecy and then presented to the Israeli people, not for approval but acceptance. During the presentation of the present agreement to the Israeli public, there was the largest demonstration in the history of Israel. Those in opposition to the so-called peace accord met in Jerusalem and virtually shut down the city for the duration of the demonstration.

The confirmed covenant of Daniel's seventieth week will be known to the world. This must be accomplished so that it will be effective, albeit short-lived. International television was the vehicle that communicated the Israeli/PLO accord to the world. Ever advancing technology will enhance the promotion of the coming peace agreement.

At the midway point (after three and a half years) of the seven-year covenant, the one-world ruler, the Antichrist, will break his peace accord with the Jewish people. This will mark the beginning of the most horrible time for God's chosen people in Jewish history. Satan and Antichrist will unleash unprecedented persecution on Israel. This period, known as the Great Tribulation, will see two of every three Jews killed (Zech. 13:8). Jesus warned Israel to flee to the wilderness for protection during this time. Jeremiah said that never has there ever been such terrible days as this three and a half years.

There are three main aspects of the Israeli/PLO agreement that are destined to cause heartache and bloodshed in the days ahead. The question of the "right of return" for the Palestinian refugees will force Israel to decide if they should open their borders to hundreds of thousands, and even millions of people who have been taught from childhood days that the Jew is on their holy land. With greater numbers of Palestinians in the land, the goal of statehood for the Palestinian people will draw these returning refugees into a more unified organization to demand statehood. With the new Palestinian state there will be the need for a capital, and from the very outset Arafat has told the world that his ambition is to see the Palestinian flag flying in the skies over Jerusalem.

These three sticky points could well trigger a terrible war in Israel that would certainly draw other Arab states sympathetic to the Palestinian cause into the fray. When you couple these problems with the ever increasing threat of Islamic fundamentalism, you have a terrible time ahead for Israel and the Jewish people.

Conclusion

The similarities between the two peace accords, Israeli/ PLO accord and the peace covenant of the Antichrist, might cause some to say the two are one and the same. Quite the contrary. Yasser Arafat does not fit the description of the coming Antichrist. Arafat does show how quickly a powerful personality could come to prominence in our world. At the point of bankruptcy, both financially and organizationally, Arafat was resurrected to prominence in only a matter of hours.

The coming conflict over returning refugees, statehood, and the status of Jerusalem will only set the stage for the coming Antichrist to step forward and claim his place of leadership according to pre-written history. The Antichrist will bring calm out of conflict. The Israeli/PLO accord is only a prerequisite for the fulfillment of Daniel 9:27.

In addition, the events of today are developing a mindset among the Jewish people and the rest of the world. This new mindset in the Jews and the world will be the preparation to usher in the prophesied events of tomorrow. God is right on schedule with His plan for the future.

The student of prophecy can rest at peace within, as he watches the events unfold that were foretold thousands of years before. Knowing God's plan for tomorrow helps you understand the activities of today. There are terrible days ahead, but the Christian can face these days with the ''blessed hope'' that he will be kept from that time of tribulation (Rev. 3:10). The Rapture, or the calling up of those who know Jesus Christ as Lord and Savior, will take place before the Daniel 9:27 peace covenant is confirmed and imposed upon the Jewish people.

With events moving as fast as they are, it is incumbent for all who claim to be saved, born-again believers in Jesus Christ to become very productive in these days. The study of prophetic truth should never encourage someone to stand on the sidelines and wait for the inevitable. Instead, these truths should be the motivation to work harder than ever before, for the night is far spent and His coming is soon.

Chapter 3

Nuclear Proliferation

Kenneth C. Hill

The buildup of nuclear armaments has been a fact of life since the nuclear arms race began in earnest after the United States dropped the first atomic bombs on Japan. Does the fact of nuclear proliferation, the wide distribution of nuclear weapons of mass destruction, cause me to believe that we are living in the last days?

The simple fact of nuclear weapons and their killing ability, along with the long-range effects of their use, do cause me to believe that we are in the last days. However, in the past few years we have seen the proliferation of such weaponry in nations that previously have not had such hardware. We now see these weapons in the hands of not only the enemies of Israel, the state (such as Russia and China), but now also in the hands of the enemies of Israel, the people of Almighty God (Islam). This certainly brings to my mind the prophecy of Ezekiel 38 and the end-time events, and causes me to believe even more strongly, if that is possible, that we are living in the last days.

Christ Himself told us that one of the signs of the end of the age is the advent of wars and the talk of wars. In Matthew 24:6-7, Christ said:

> *"And ye shall hear of wars and rumours of*
> *wars: see that ye be not troubled: for all these*

things must come to pass, but the end is not yet.
For nation shall rise against nation, and king-
dom against kingdom: and there shall be fam-
ines, and pestilences, and earthquakes, in divers
places.''

In Mark 13:7 Christ said,

''And when ye shall hear of wars and rumours
of wars, be ye not troubled: for such things
must needs be; but the end shall not be yet.''

The story of mankind is a story of bloodshed, murder, and wars. About this fact, N.W. Hutchings wrote:

''. . . Man has fought 4,535 wars. . . . Some
people say, in regard to this particular sign of
the end of the age, 'Oh, we have always had
war.' However, Jesus was stressing that at the
time liars and deceivers would increase, and
an unusual number of false christs would
arise, there would be a corresponding rise in
the number and intensity of wars. Keep in mind
that in all of history, six hundred million
people have been killed in wars which oc-
curred in the twentieth century. In other words,
there have been as many people killed in war
since 1914 as in the previous fifty-five hundred
years. World War I and World War II eclipsed
all previous wars in intensity, scope, and de-
struction. Today, without success, our diplo-
mats are working feverishly to prevent World
War III. It is evident that when Jesus spoke of
nation rising against nation and kingdom
against kingdom, He was not simply declaring

the obvious, but pointing to something that
would occur at the end of the age.'' [1]

What about the nuclear threat and its effect upon the
wars that are happening about us and the wars yet to come?
Some researchers downplay the problem of the wide distribution of nuclear weaponry contending that the nuclear threat,
although increased by the dissolution of the former Soviet
Union, is nothing to worry about. They contend that

''. . . missile proliferation is no worse a phe-
nomenon than the proliferation of other less
glamorous weapons.'' [2]

The argument does make sense and should remind us
that other ''less glamorous'' weapons (chemical, biological,
other types of non-nuclear munitions) must be taken into
account when we consider the end-time truth of the increase of
wars and the talk of wars.

In the research to date, it is alarming to see the increase
in the number of nations that have become members of the once
exclusive ''nuclear weapons club.'' It is acknowledged that
France, Britain, the former Soviet Union, China, and the United
States have long been members of the club. Now we must add
Israel, Pakistan, India, North Korea, and South Africa.[3] Another group of nations has moved into the ''perhaps or almost''
members of the club, including Iraq, Iran, Algeria, Turkey,
Syria, and Libya.[4,5] These are nations who either now have, or
are working hard to have, their own nuclear weapons industry.
These plan not to be mere players in the game, but to have the
capability to supply nuclear armaments for their own uses and
the use of their allies and business partners.

China is busy selling its weapons around the world.

''The Chinese have been selling ballistic mis-

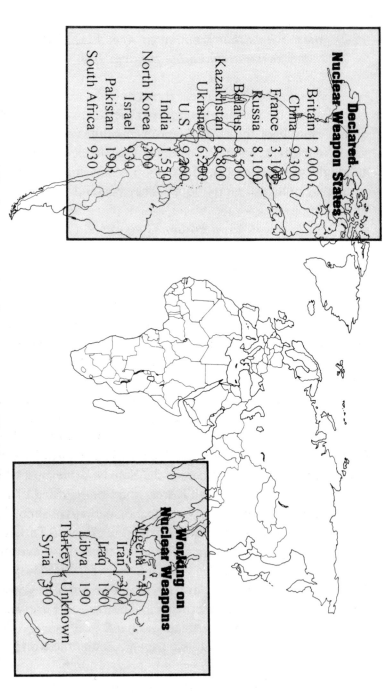

Declared Nuclear Weapon States

Britain	2,000
China	9,300
France	3,100
Russia	8,100
Belarus	6,500
Kazakhstan	6,800
Ukraine	6,200
U.S.	9,200
India	1,550
North Korea	300
Israel	930
Pakistan	190
South Africa	930

Working on Nuclear Weapons

Algeria	40
Iran	300
Iraq	190
Libya	190
Turkey	Unknown
Syria	300

* Numbers represent nuclear weapons quantities in each country.

*siles and nuclear equipment to all comers.
. . . Pakistan, Saudia Arabia, and Iran. . . .
China is getting new missile technology from
Russia and Ukraine.''* [6]

China has been compared to an old-style Western arms trader of conventional weapons, except these are nuclear weapons of mass destruction. The Chinese see the trade in nuclear weapons as a lucrative business and seem not to care about the consequences for themselves or the rest of the world.

In one of the former Soviet republics, the Ukraine, there are at least thirty nuclear bombers, one hundred and seventy-six strategic missiles, and sixteen hundred warheads that they want to keep for protection against the Russian republic should Russia want to take over their government again. The real fear is that by late 1994 the Ukrainians may be able to re-direct the missiles and targeting devices that are presently unchangeable. They will do this by

*''. . . cracking the Russian computer codes that
prevent Kiev from retargeting or firing the
nuclear missiles itself. . . . They will gain
operational control of the world's third largest
stockpile of nuclear weapons. Moscow has not
explicitly told the U.S. that it might attack
Ukraine to prevent Kiev from obtaining control, but they have hinted at very high levels
that this could happen.'' [7]*

Those in the former Soviet Union have not been silent about the situation within their republics. Russian president Boris Yeltsin was featured in an *Izvestia* story under the headline ''Cold War Is Over, But There Are No Fewer 'Hot Spots.''' [8] *Izvestia* carried an article in January 1992, under the headline ''Bombs Cannot Be Made at Soviet Nuclear Centers

Abroad--But Our Specialists Can Fill In the Gap,'' which stated in part,

> "*. . . Libya has always paid cash and never asked for credits. . . . Soviet (nuclear) research centers have been built in Egypt and Vietnam, and projects have been drawn up for Syria and Cuba.*''[9]

Arms Control Today reported in December 1991, more than sixty former Soviet nuclear-weapons scientists were working in Brazil, India, Iran, Iraq, and Pakistan.

Meanwhile, *Pravda* carried a statement of the Ministry of Foreign Affairs of the Republic of Kazakhstan in its January 30, 1992, edition denying any decision of that republic to sell nuclear weaponry.[10] Incidents of soldiers searching for drugs at roadblocks in Russia and finding stolen nuclear weapons parts are common. The Italian press has reported that Soviet nuclear-tipped artillery shells have been offered for sale in Italy.[11]

The Bulletin for Atomic Scientists has reported that of the former Soviet nuclear arsenal, ninety-five percent of the weapons are in four republics. Seventy percent are in Russia, fifteen percent are in the Ukraine, seven percent are in Kazakhstan, and five percent are in Belarus. The Caucasus republics (Georgia, Armenia, Azerbaijan) have three percent, and the central Asian republics (Turkmenistan, Uzbekistan, Tajikistan, and Kirghizia) have less than two percent. Not included in this accounting are the comparatively few weapons in the countries of Lithuania, Latvia, and Estonia.[12] Azerbaijan, Kazakhstan, Uzbekistan, Kirghizia, Turkmenistan, and Tajikistan are Muslim nations that hold approximately ten percent of the former Soviet Union's nuclear arsenal.

Why is this a special threat? Perhaps an excerpt from the Southwest Radio Church booklet, *Islam Encroaches*, will help our understanding of this special concern.

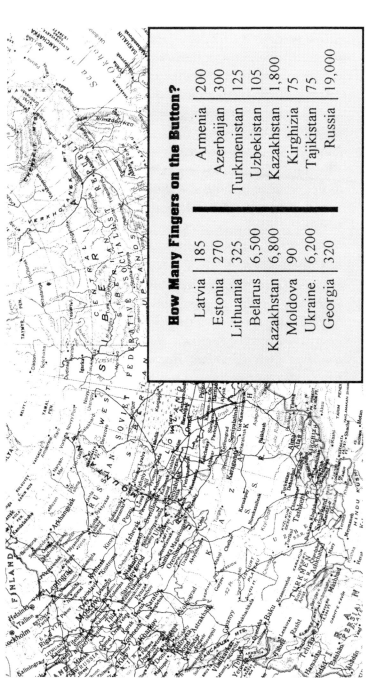

How Many Fingers on the Button?

Latvia	185	Armenia	200
Estonia	270	Azerbaijan	300
Lithuania	325	Turkmenistan	125
Belarus	6,500	Uzbekistan	105
Kazakhstan	6,800	Kazakhstan	1,800
Moldova	90	Kirghizia	75
Ukraine.	6,200	Tajikistan	75
Georgia	320	Russia	19,000

* **Numbers represent nuclear weapons quantities in each country.**

"The prophet of Islam, Muhammad, killed thousands and perhaps hundreds of thousands, yet Jesus Christ, nor one of His apostles or disciples, killed anyone. . . . Muslims strive to be more like Muhammad, even as Christians should strive to be more like Jesus Christ. . . . Islamic . . . terrorists are at work in Sudan, Ethiopia, Egypt, Libya, Israel, the United States, and many other nations around the world. Iraq now has nuclear weapons that have been purchased from the Islamic nations that broke off from the Soviet Union. Iran now has missiles that will reach Israel. What would happen if a terrorist group would demand the surrender of the government of the United States on the grounds that a nuclear bomb was in a van parked between the National Capital Building and the White House? Statements from informed military sources reflect concern about this possible danger. . . .

"The Soviet Empire has ended, but a new empire seems to be rising from its ashes. The new empire is not the new commonwealth or the former Russian republic--the new empire is the great Islamic wave.

"Amazing events are occurring in our world today, especially in the Muslim world. . . . Never before in history have world events changed more suddenly or dramatically from the perspective of Bible prophecy. Never have so many biblically relevant factors converged more clearly.

"The former southern republics of the Soviet Union are all Muslim nations except the Ukraine, Armenia, and Georgia. . . . The fall

of the Soviet Union has spawned the existence of six new, powerful independent Muslim nations.

"These newly independent nations have three main things in common. First, as already noted, they are all Muslim. Second, they all lack hard currency. Third, they have nuclear weapons within their boundaries and at their disposal. These three factors are obviously a dangerous combination. The scenario is clear: these six republics will conspire with their Islamic brothers in Iran, Syria, Pakistan, Libya, and Turkey to exchange nuclear devices for hard currency. The common bond that binds them together is their common commitment to destroy Israel.

"Experts on Middle East affairs are proclaiming a powerful new surge in militant Islam in the Middle East. Judith Miller says, '. . . Militant Islam is once again on the move, shaking the foundations of culture and government in even the most stable Arab states. . . . More than a decade after the first modern Islamic revolution, in Iran, militant Islam is . . . transforming everyday life in the Middle East and challenging the legitimacy of almost every state.

"So what is the cause of this sudden rise in militant Islam? Experts agree that two explosive events in the last year have served as catalysts for the new rise in Islam. The two events are the Persian Gulf war and the collapse of the Soviet Union and communism.

"Communism was the strongest opponent to militant Islam in the Middle East.

Therefore, the fall of the Soviet Union and communism have thrown the door wide open for militant Islam to rise like a shooting star in the Middle East.

"The breakup of the Soviet Union has caused a dramatic power shift that affects every area of the world. The world has not been stabilized by the fall of the Soviet Union; it has been greatly destabilized. . . . The world is more at risk for a global holocaust than at any time in history. Nuclear weapons are being distributed and are falling into the hands of irrational, fanatical leaders! The foment in the Islamic world could ignite at any time into a jihad, *or holy war. . . .*

"Islam has emerged as the world's fastest growing religion, with over one billion followers. . . . Today there are more Muslims in Great Britain than Christians. Over nine hundred churches have been converted into mosques. In the United States there are over three million Muslims. There are more followers of Islam in the United States than Episcopalians, and three times more Muslims than members of the Assemblies of God.

"All of the Muslim former republics of the Soviet Union are being courted by their Islamic neighbors--especially Turkey and Iran. Most importantly, however, is the fact that all of these former republics have tactical nuclear weapons within their boundaries, except Kirghizia, and Kazakhstan has not only tactical nuclear weapons, but also ICBM (intercontinental ballistic missile) sites and strategic bomber bases. Some have ranked

Kazakhstan as the fourth greatest nuclear power in the world today.

". . . Many of the younger generation of radicals accuse the official Islamic establishment of having collaborated with the godless Soviet regime. These radicals have made their view very clear: ' "It doesn't matter that they are Shiite over there, and we Sunni," argues a militant in the Uzbek city of Namangan. "The Ayatollah made Iran strong and glorious, while in Sunni Turkey they have weakened Islam." Muslim political aspirations have found a focus in the Islamic Renaissance Party, which held its founding congress in 1990. . . . "Our goals are similar to those of the Iranian revolution. . . . We stand for tradition." '

"This new militant political party now has chapters in both Uzbekistan and Tajikistan. In another city in Uzbekistan, so many people stream to the mosques during the afternoon prayer that Islamic guards must be used to keep order. The cry that echoes from these mosques is 'God is great!'

"One political expert in this area says, 'The growth of the Islamic movement will be in direct proportion to the decline in the region's economic and social conditions. . . . If the West waits until tomorrow or the day after to get involved, it may be too late.'

"In other words, if economic conditions get too bad, these nations are an Islamic powder keg waiting to explode. With the world's economy like it is today, it's very likely that the fuse to this powder keg is already burning!" [13]

The proliferation of nuclear weapons is a major threat to world peace. The United States, the greatest nuclear power, cannot prevent the coming wars. As *Time* magazine recently reported,

> *"However firm its stance, the U.S. cannot eliminate the ambitions and fears that prod nations to acquire weapons of mass destruction. Washington could not guarantee Arab states against Israel, India against China, Pakistan against India, or Iran against Iraq. Some of them have the bomb now, and the others will get it. In coming years, the U.S. will have to choose very carefully where to engage its interests and its military forces. It may have its hands full just protecting itself."* [14]

This proliferation of nuclear weapons and the outfitting of the former Soviet Islamic republics with such weapons fits directly into the outline of Ezekiel 38 where we read from portions of that chapter:

> *"Son of man, set thy face against Gog, the land of Magog, the chief prince of Meshech and Tubal, and prophesy against him, And say, Thus saith the Lord God; Behold, I am against thee, O Gog, the chief prince of Meshech and Tubal: And I will turn thee back, and put hooks into thy jaws, and I will bring thee forth, and all thine army, horses and horsemen, all of them clothed with all sorts of armour, even a great company with bucklers and shields, all of them handling swords: Persia, Ethiopia, and Libya with them; all of them with shield and helmet: Gomer, and all his bands; the house of*

Togarmah of the north quarters, and all his bands: and many people with thee. . . . Thus saith the Lord God; It shall also come to pass, that at the same time shall things come into thy mind, and thou shalt think an evil thought: And thou shalt say, I will go up to the land of unwalled villages; I will go to them that are at rest, that dwell safely, all of them dwelling without walls, and having neither bars nor gates, To take a spoil, and to take a prey; to turn thine hand upon the desolate places that are now inhabited, and upon the people that are gathered out of the nations, which have gotten cattle and goods, that dwell in the midst of the land. . . . Therefore, son of man, prophesy and say unto Gog, Thus saith the Lord God; In that day when my people of Israel dwelleth safely, shalt thou not know it? And thou shalt come from thy place out of the north parts, thou, and many people with thee, all of them riding upon horses, a great company, and a mighty army: And thou shalt come up against my people of Israel, as a cloud to cover the land; it shall be in the latter days, and I will bring thee against my land, that the heathen may know me, when I shall be sanctified in thee, O Gog, before their eyes'' (Ezek. 38:2-6,10-12,14-16).

The proliferation of the nuclear weapons reminds us that the return of Jesus Christ is very soon. We are living in the last days. Are you ready? The follower of Christ Jesus has the blessed hope of His soon appearing.

Are *you* ready? *You* can be.

Romans 3:23 tells us that we are all sinners. We have

all missed the mark of goodness and the standard that God has set for us. We have been judged as a sinner and must die, as it says in Romans 6:23 that the wages, what we earn in our sin, is death! That death is eternal separation from God in a place of torment and pain, called the Lake of Fire.

But there is hope, because the last part of Romans 6:23 tells us that God's gift to you is eternal life, not death.

Romans 10:9-10,13 promises,

> *"That if thou shalt confess with thy mouth the Lord Jesus, and shalt believe in thine heart that God hath raised him from the dead, thou shalt be saved. For with the heart man believeth unto righteousness; and with the mouth confession is made unto salvation. . . . For whosoever shall call upon the name of the Lord shall be saved."*

Ephesians 2:8-10 says,

> *"For by grace are ye saved through faith; and that not of yourselves: it is the gift of God: Not of works, lest any man should boast. For we are his workmanship, created in Christ Jesus unto good works, which God hath before ordained that we should walk in them."*

Will you receive the gift of eternal life through Christ's finished work on the cross for you?

If you are a follower of Jesus Christ, are you ready? What sort of person should you be, seeing that Christ's call for His Church is very near? Be about the Father's business! Even as you are told in Ephesians 2:10, you are God's handiwork and have been created in our Lord Jesus Christ to do God's good works until Jesus returns! Even so, come, Lord Jesus!

Notes

1. *Understanding Problem Prophetic Passages*, Vol. I, Noah W. Hutchings; Hearthstone Publishing, Ltd., Oklahoma City, OK; 1991; pp. 19-20.
2. *ORBIS*, Winter 1991, "How Much Does Missile Proliferation Matter?" Uzi Rubin; p. 37.
3, 4. *Foreign Affairs*, Fall 1992, "The New Nuclear Threat," John M. Deutch; p. 118.
5. *Time*, June 21, 1992, "Fighting Off Doomsday," Bruce W. Nelan; p. 38.
6. *Ibid*, p. 37
7. *Ibid*
8, 9. *The Current Digest of the Soviet Press*, February 26, 1992, "Arms Control"; p. 19.
10. *Ibid*, p. 20.
11. *CO Researcher*, June 5, 1992, "Nuclear Proliferation: The Issues," Rodman D. Griffan; p. 483.
12. *Bulletin of the Atomic Scientist*, November 1991, "Where the Weapons Are," Robert S. Norris; pp. 48-49.
13. *Islam Encroaches*, David A. Ingraham, Noah W. Hutchings, and Mark Hitchcock; Southwest Radio Church, Oklahoma City, OK; 1993; pp. 13-18.
14. *Time*, June 21, 1992, "Fighting Off Doomsday," Bruce W. Nelan; p. 38.

Chapter Four

THE NEW WORLD ORDER

Dr. Ray W. Yerbury
D.B.S., M.A., B.Th., B.Ecom., Dip.Ind.Chem.

When God created the world, He intended to be its ruler. However, He gave His created being man the privilege of choice. Surrounded by a perfect environment and paradise called the Garden of Eden, mankind succumbed to the temptation of Satan and from that point in history he has always thought he could do a better job than God.

He has relentlessly usurped God's authority. He has desired his own human government, with kings and rulers and leaders. Man has sought to build empires and become master of the universe where today, almost six thousand years after the fall, we now live in a generation where there is an almost all consuming quest for a Utopian world, guided by a central authority and under the leadership of a popular charismatic Messiah. But to the majority of people, it does not take a university degree to realize that the world is not getting better, as many would persuade us to believe, but rather our universe is in the process of having a giant hemorrhage.

The great Jewish/American physicist, Albert Einstein, once admitted that mankind's desire for peace can be realized only by the creation of a world government.

Two years after the end of World War II, British statesman Sir Winston Churchill declared:

> "*Unless some effective world super-govern-*
> *ment can be set up and brought quickly into*

*action, the prospects for peace and human
progress are indeed dark and doubtful."*

Many groups are emerging offering hope in a world
gone mad. The New Age movement, with its roots firmly
planted in Eastern Hindu mysticism, promotes "mind science"
and the concept of the "Age of Aquarius" or "a New World
Order" as the only way of salvation for the world. They say the
New Age Christ, or "Lord Maitreya," will soon appear to lead
the world into the twenty-first century--but they said that in the
year 1982, and we are still waiting for him to emerge from his
hiding place!

. . . And so the world continues to cry out: What is the
solution to the inflation problem, unemployment, crime wave,
drug addiction, pollution, sexual immorality, armament buildup? The question as to who is to blame for the existing
conditions echoes and re-echoes in the news media with
monotonous regularity. It's popular to blame the politicians,
after all, it's their job to solve our woes, but do they really care?

There is unrest among the youth of our nation. They
believe that the national leaders are too old and incompetent.
The more mature leaders are blaming the education system for
a restless youth, and so the blame ebbs to and fro across the sea
of indecision and no one is really prepared to take the scalpel
and operate on the real cause of the cancer in our society, a
small word that has created a gigantic problem since creation,
and that is *sin*.

During the 1900s we have seen as never before rapid
changes in world conditions. Governments have risen and
fallen almost overnight. Wars and uprisings deploying high
technology were won or lost within weeks. The catch cry of a
"New World Order" is heard every day by our national
leaders.

It was reported that during the early days of Saddam
Hussein's rise to world notoriety, President Bush's decisive

move to blunt Iraq's aggression in the Middle East began to shape a brave new world order. At the same time, on the other side of the globe, Eduard Shevardnadze, who was then the foreign minister during Mikhail Gorbachev's reign, was quoted in the December 31, 1990 *Time* magazine as saying,

> *"Dictatorship is coming. . . . No one knows what this dictatorship will be like, what kind of dictator will come to power and what order will be established."* [2]

More recently, the Palestine Liberation Organization (PLO) chief Yasser Arafat, in an interview for the German news weekly *Der Speigel*, and commenting particularly on the PLO-Israeli autonomy pact signed in Washington, D.C. in September 1993, said that the accord was

> *". . . the best that could be achieved given current relations in the Arab world, and the new world order."* [3]

Global Rule—The Next Step?

Former Soviet leader Mikhail Gorbachev has been calling for the creation of a new world order or global government for many years. After receiving an honorary doctorate from Westminster College in Fulton, Missouri, Mr. Gorbachev spoke from the same podium where, in 1946, Winston Churchill gave his historic "iron curtain" address that marked the beginning of the Cold War. Forty-six years later, Mr. Gorbachev symbolically buried the conflict with his call for world democracy. *"The United Nations could take on the role of a world government,"* Gorbachev said. He also proposed that Germany and Japan be admitted to the Security Council as permanent members. [4]

When one scans the editorial columns of the major

newspapers from western developed countries, one cannot help but notice a common thread that weaves its pattern in the minds of thinking people concerned about saving humanity from what now seems to be overwhelming problems. Almost without exception the catch-cry is "global government." The nations of the world have been moving tentatively toward a worldwide political administrative system since the founding of the League of Nations. But both the league and its successor, the U.N., did not save humanity from war and other global afflictions, simply because the nations failed to abandon the fetish of absolute "state sovereignty." However, with our planet's problems becoming increasingly threatening, many people are coming to recognize the vital requirements of forming a global government which has the power to transcend state sovereignty so that it can set and enforce international laws.

 . . . But this global government--the "New World Order"--is being set up on man's terms and by man's action. Bible prophecy, however, does confirm that it will happen. There will be a world government, ruled by the most ruthless of dictators--a man known as the "son of destruction"--the Antichrist of the end-time seven year Tribulation period.

What Does the Bible Say About a New World Order?

The Old Testament book of Daniel 8, together with the last book of the Bible--Revelation 13, 17, and 18--inform us that during the latter days there will be a one world religious and commercial system on this earth. The Word of God also tells us that there is a "New World Order" coming, but this final one will be ushered in not by man, but by Almighty God. The book of Daniel makes it quite clear as to the nature of the new order.

"And in the days of these kings shall the God of heaven set up a kingdom, which shall never be destroyed: and the kingdom shall not be left

to other people, but it shall break in pieces and consume all these kingdoms, and it shall stand for ever'' (Dan. 2:44).

New World Order or World Control?

Revelation 13:7,16-18 has this to say:

''And it was given unto him to make war with the saints, and to overcome them: and power was given him over all kindreds, and tongues, and nations. . . . And he causeth all, both small and great, rich and poor, free and bond, to receive a mark in their right hand, or in their foreheads: And that no man might buy or sell, save he that had the mark, or the name of the beast, or the number of his name. Here is wisdom. Let him that hath understanding count the number of the beast: for it is the number of a man; and his number is Six hundred three-score and six.''

The picture painted in this reading from the book of Revelation is drawn from the Tribulation period. The true Church or believers have gone to be with the Lord (1 Thess. 4:13-18; 1 Cor. 15:51-54), thus allowing the Beast or world dictator to be revealed (2 Thess. 2:7). This dictator, also known as the Antichrist, achieves such control as indicated by the authority he has over the whole world, controlling people economically as well as politically.

The first world dictator recorded in the Bible was Nimrod, the builder of Babylon. During his reign, mankind, who had emerged from the ark, attempted to build a tower to heaven. God, however, judged this an attempt at internationalism and scattered mankind, dividing them by languages.

The Start of a Modern New World Order or One-Worldism

In modern times the Illuminati founded by Professor Adam Weishaupt on May 1, 1776 was the first attempt at international control. The aims of this organization can be summarized in the following six points:

a. Abolition of monarchy and all structured government;

b. Abolition of private property and resources;

c. Abolition of private wealth and inheritance;

d. Abolition of patriotism;

e. Abolition of the family;

f. Abolition of religion and its replacement with reason.

The Illuminati played a major role in the French Revolution of 1789-94, using the ''Jacobin Club'' as their vehicle. They called for a new world order and a universal republic. In 1847 a new Illuminati society called the Communist League was formed. This group commissioned a Jew by the name of Karl Marx to write the *Communist Manifesto* in 1848. The communists adopted the six points of the Illuminati doctrine. Ironically, one hundred years later in 1948, the modern state of Israel was established on the strength of the U.S.S.R. to vote in the United Nations.

In 1891 Cecil Rhodes, who through his will founded the Rhodes Scholarship scheme, devoted his fortune to promoting his lifelong dream of a new world order and a world government, establishing a secret society known as the Round Table Group. International bankers such as Lord Rothschild were involved in the society from its inception.

Enter the Club of Rome

A group of one hundred men from at least twenty-five

nations came together to form this group in 1957. Their leader, Dr. Peccei, stated:

> *"The only possible way to make decisions is to take a global approach. A New International Order will have to be established not just in the economic sphere, but in social and political areas."*

The Club of Rome divided the world into ten segments.

1. North America
2. Western Europe
3. Japan
4. Israel, South Africa, and Australia
5. Eastern Europe, including Russia
6. Latin America
7. North Africa and Middle East
8. Main Africa
9. South and Southeast Asia
10. Central Asia, including China

The club's solution to international problems were:

1. A global approach to the problem;
2. Investment aid rather than commodity aid, with the exception being food;
3. Balanced economic development in all regions;
4. Effective population policies;
5. Worldwide diversification of industry.

Very little has been heard of the Club of Rome during recent times. However, it is still a very influential worldwide organization that is reputedly working for the solving of the major problems of the world. It promotes the concept of world government and global strategy.

At their annual conference, held in Kuala Lumpur in November 1992, some eighty participants from thirty countries on the five continents adopted the following final declaration:

> *"We are entering a totally new society which is characterized by globalization and at the same time by cultural pluralism. Interdependence between nations, gaps between the richest and the poorest countries, and a number of environmental threats mark the present situation. In facing this new emerging global society with deep changes affecting the world after the collapse of communism and the implosion of the U.S.S.R., with rapid demographic growth in the south, and aging population in the north, the global community will have to be innovative because of the magnitude and the novelty of the problem awaiting to be solved. We are certainly not yet equipped to embark on this new society with our traditional mentalities, behavior, and archaic institutional structures. The aim is toward the construction of new systems of governance with the main object of a better world order."* [5]

Can the United Nations Solve Our Problems?

More recently, the United Nations has become center stage for the dramatic events now unfolding before our eyes. Its secretary-general, Egypt's Boutros-Ghali, has asked that the U.N. be given its own world army. Global peace, says Boutros-Ghali, can only come from the mouth of a gun and from the fiery exhaust of an aircraft missile.

Calls keep ringing out across the globe imploring the U.N. to use its armed might and firepower to put down local insurgencies, rebellions, and violations. Some have suggested in the wake of the 1992 Earth Summit conference held in Rio de Janeiro, that the U.N. be given authority to police the globe punishing polluters and levying fines on "guilty" global citizens. Could this not be the beginning of the "enviro-cops" of planet earth?

Recently three American presidents--Clinton, Bush, and Reagan--delivered major speeches calling for the creation of a world army to be controlled by the United Nations. Was this a mere coincidence or the result of a contrived plot to set up a global government?

Texe Marrs (a leading prophetic researcher, teacher, and writer in the U.S.) says the Council of Foreign Relations, the Trilateral Commission, and the World Federalists, under the direction of the Bilderbergers, are conspiring to terminate American sovereignty and deliver the United States' Armed Forces into the hands of a U.N. bureaucracy.

The ruthless Rockefeller and Rothschild banking and oil combines have worked behind the scenes to set up a global government based on occult principles. Russia's dictators-- first Lenin, Gorbachev, and now Yelstin--have for decades slavishly cooperated with the Rockerfeller-Rothschild forces.

The time for the U.N. to become a real world government, complete with its own blue beret army, an I.R.S. taxing authority, and a global intelligence service, is now at hand!

The Secret Brotherhood fully expects that their spectacular plot will succeed in all its dark glory by the end of the year 1999. They are convinced that all of humanity is soon to fall under their thumbs. [6]

The Two Riders on a White Horse
The book of Revelation reveals not one but two riders on white horses. In Revelation 19:11,16 we read:

"And I saw heaven opened, and behold a white horse; and he that sat upon him was called Faithful and True, and in righteousness he doth judge and make war. . . . And he hath on his vesture and on his thigh a name written, KING OF KINGS, AND LORD OF LORDS."

There can be no doubt as to the identity of this symbolic horseman, for there is only one who could claim to be the King of kings and Lord of lords, and that is Jesus Christ. In this chapter we have the picture of the second coming of Jesus Christ to planet earth to set up His earthly kingdom and to reign for one thousand years. However, before that great and wonderful event, the first rider on a white horse appears on earth and we find reference to this personage in Revelation 6:2

"And I saw, and behold a white horse: and he that sat on him had a bow; and a crown was given unto him: and he went forth conquering, and to conquer."

In point of fact, there are four horsemen in this chapter. The rider on the white horse is followed in rapid succession by the riders of the red, black, and pale horses. This imagery of horses is a symbolic representation of false peace, wars, bloodshed, famine, pestilence, diseases, and death. This is the image of the global terror that is to come during the last days just prior to Christ's glorious return.

Now returning to the rider on the white horse as outlined in Revelation 6. Note that he rides a white horse with a crown on his head and holds a bow in his hand. This indicates that he will be almost universally admired as a peacemaker, a savior or messiah, who comes to rescue humanity from the severe crisis and insoluble problems which will confront the world during the last days.

The passage in Revelation also informs us that this rider has a bow, but there is no mention of arrows. This would seem to indicate that he has the military means to enforce peace. The fact that he wears a crown tells us that he will be accorded the political power necessary to fulfill his global role as a conqueror.

There is little doubt that we are living today in a hostile environment. Men and women everywhere are crying out for a leader, a hero, a statesman to put things right--a man on a white horse--a charismatic leader at the helm of a global organization. The stage has now been set for the rider on the white horse to come forward and take his ominous place on the stage of human history. The planet and its people have been conditioned. All is ready. It's time!

What Is God's Purpose for the World?

Isaiah the prophet, from whom Jesus loved to quote, had this to say about the purpose of this world:

> "*God himself that formed the earth and made it; he hath established it, he created it not in vain, he formed it to be inhabited: I am the Lord; and there is none else*" (Isa. 45:18).

This is comforting that the earth is to be inhabited and not to become a desert void as pictured by the scare mongers of space fiction. Again Isaiah declares:

> "*for the earth shall be full of the knowledge of the Lord, as the waters cover the sea*" (Isa. 11:9).

> "*. . . when thy judgments are in the earth, the inhabitants of the world will learn righteousness*" (Isa. 26:9).

Now ideas like the *"knowledge of the Lord and righteousness"* do not rate very high among the people of the world today. Nevertheless, whether the people of this world like it or not, *there is* a *New World Order* coming . . . not the Bush's or Gorbachev's new world brought about by man's action, but by what God is going to do, because in the book of Revelation it also says:

> " . . . *The kingdoms of this world are become the kingdoms of our Lord, and of his Christ; and he shall reign for ever and ever"* (Rev. 11:15).

When Will This Utopian World (N.W.O.) Come Into Being?

After the Rapture of believers. At the conclusion of the judgments: the Bema Judgment, Tribulation judgments, the Judgment of the Nations. After the Marriage Supper of the Lamb in Heaven--at the *Second Coming of Christ* to this earth who will set up His throne and reign for one thousand years. Refer to Chart 1.

> ". . . *the Lord God shall give unto him the throne of his father David: And he shall reign over the house of Jacob for ever; and of his kingdom there shall be no end"* (Luke 1:32-33).

Some Scholars Take a Different View of the Millennium

There are a number of schools of thought regarding the one thousand year period often referred to as "the Millennium." Some don't even believe in a literal, physical reign of Jesus Christ on this earth. Refer to Charts 2 and 3.

The word *Millennium* does not occur in the Bible as

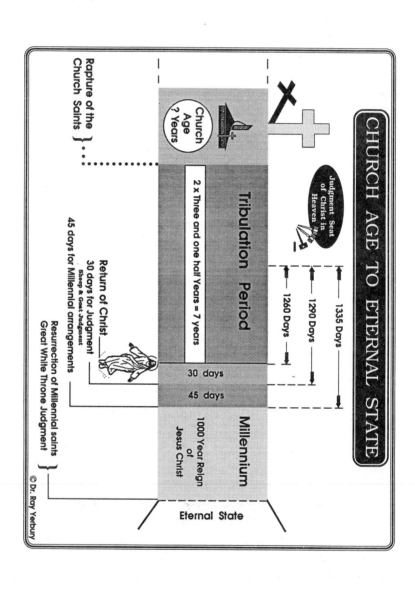

CHURCH AGE TO ETERNAL STATE

Rapture of the Church Saints

Church Age ? Years

Judgment Seat of Christ in Heaven

Tribulation Period

2 x Three and one half Years = 7 years

1335 Days
1290 Days
1260 Days

30 days

45 days

Return of Christ
30 days for Judgment
Sheep & Goat Judgment
45 days for Millennial arrangements

Resurrection of Millennial saints
Great White Throne Judgment

Millennium

1000 Year Reign of Jesus Christ

Eternal State

© Dr. Ray Yerbury

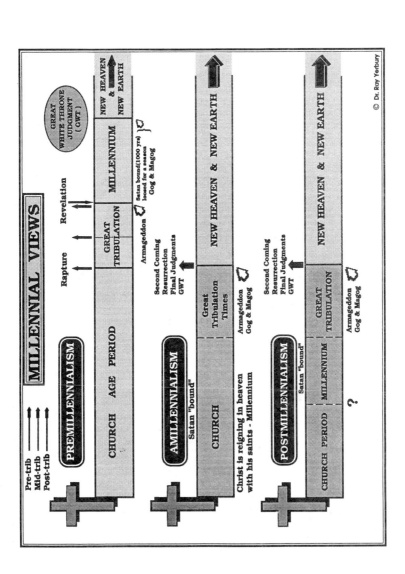

MILLENNIAL VIEWS

Pre-trib
Mid-trib
Post-trib

Rapture   Revelation

GREAT
WHITE THRONE
JUDGMENT
(GWT)

PREMILLENNIALISM

CHURCH   AGE   PERIOD

GREAT
TRIBULATION

MILLENNIUM

NEW HEAVEN
&
NEW EARTH

Armageddon

Satan bound(1000 yrs)
loosed for a season
Gog & Magog

AMILLENNIALISM
Satan "bound"

CHURCH

Christ is reigning in heaven
with his saints - Millennium

Great
Tribulation
Times

Armageddon
Gog & Magog

Second Coming
Resurrection
Final Judgments
GWT

NEW HEAVEN & NEW EARTH

POSTMILLENNIALISM
Satan "bound"

CHURCH PERIOD

MILLENNIUM

?

GREAT
TRIBULATION

Armageddon
Gog & Magog

Second Coming
Resurrection
Final Judgments
GWT

NEW HEAVEN & NEW EARTH

© Dr. Roy Yerbury

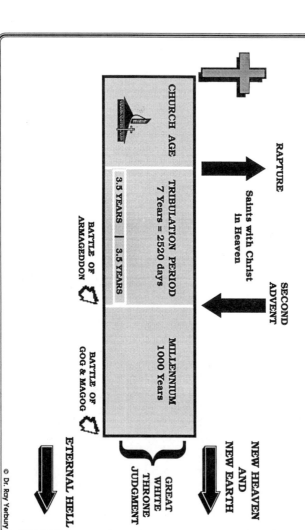

PREMILLENNIAL SCHEME OF WORLD EVENTS

CHURCH AGE

RAPTURE

Saints with Christ
In Heaven

SECOND
ADVENT

TRIBULATION PERIOD
7 Years = 2520 days

3.5 YEARS | 3.5 YEARS

BATTLE OF
ARMAGEDDON

MILLENNIUM
1000 Years

BATTLE OF
GOG & MAGOG

GREAT
WHITE
THRONE
JUDGMENT

NEW HEAVEN
AND
NEW EARTH

ETERNAL HELL

© Dr. Roy Yerbury

such. It comes from the Latin words *mille* and *ehhum*, meaning "one thousand" and "years." The one thousand years' reign of Christ is mentioned six times, and only in chapter 20 of the book of Revelation.

Pre-Millennialists have often been criticized for basing their belief in a literal Millennium entirely on one chapter in a book that is noted for its frequent use of symbols. However, that is hardly a valid criticism, as we are about to clearly demonstrate. This New World Order-Millennial Reign of Jesus Christ will commence with the physical, visible, and literal presence of Christ in Jerusalem, Israel.

The reason that there must be a physical reign on this earth is because of the covenant with Abraham as recorded in Genesis 12,13,15, and 17. It was an unconditional covenant given by God to Abraham involving land and people, and it was to be an everlasting covenant.

Who Will Live In This Millennial Kingdom?

The campaign of Armageddon as described in Revelation 19; Joel 3; and Zechariah 12 and 14 is now over. The great union of saved Gentiles and Jews has taken place at the Marriage Supper of the Lamb in God's heavenly realm. Jesus Christ has flung open the windows of heaven; has traveled down the stairways of the stars, and now emerges into the wide expanse of His Millennial Kingdom to reign on this earth for one thousand years, and then finally, with the Father in the eternal state forever and forever.

In Jude 14 we have prophecy's *first word* from man:

> "*And Enoch also, the seventh from Adam, prophesied of these, saying, Behold, the Lord cometh with ten thousands of his saints.*"

Question: Who Are These Holy Ones?

Now identification of these "holy ones" will give us

the clues as to who will occupy the Millennial Kingdom on planet earth in their glorified bodies. I believe Scripture indicates at least five distinct groups:

1. **Angels**: *"For the Son of man shall come in the glory of his Father with his angels; and then he shall reward every man according to his works"* (Matt. 16:27). *"And he saith unto him, Verily, verily, I say unto you, Hereafter ye shall see heaven open, and the angels of God ascending and descending upon the Son of man"* (John 1:51).

2. **All Believers of the Church Age:** All believers who die prior to the Rapture of the true Church. Philippians 1:21-23 indicates that at the death all believers go directly to heaven but remain in a ''soulish state'' awaiting the resurrection. They will receive their glorified body first in accordance with 1 Thessalonians 4:16. Then, we who are alive will be raptured and immediately receive our glorified body (1 Cor. 15:53) *"Behold, he cometh with clouds; and every eye shall see him, and they also which pierced him: and all kindreds of the earth shall wail because of him. Even so, Amen"* (Rev. 1:7).

    What are the clouds? They are the Bride of Christ, the glorified believers clothed in fine linen, bright and clean, which speaks of the righteousness of the saints (Rev. 19:8).

3. **Martyred Saints:** Those who are saved during the first half of the Tribulation as a result of the witness of the hundred and forty-four thousand Jewish evangelists (Rev. 7:13-17). They apparently serve the Lord before the Throne forever.

4. **Sealed Jews:** The one hundred and forty-four thousand from Revelation 7 are the same group as in Revelation 14. They are now seen standing with the Lamb on heavenly Mount Zion. How did they get there? They were *raptured* (caught up together at the conclusion of their evangelistic ministry on earth) at the mid-Tribulation point.

5. **Old Testament Saints:** Immediately after the description of

the Tribulation in Daniel 11, deliverance is now promised to Israel at the close of the Tribulation as outlined in Daniel 12. The Old Testament saints are the invited guests to the marriage supper (Rev. 19:9), which will occur just prior to Christ's glorious appearing.

The Sequence of Events When Christ Comes

1. **He will come with His saints to** *Jerusalem* (Zech. 14:4-9).
2. **Satan will be "locked and sealed"** in the abyss by an ordinary angel to keep him from deceiving the nations anymore, until the one thousand years are ended (Rev. 20:3).
3. **There is a** *"first resurrection"* (Rev. 20:4-6). For all those who have died as a witness for Christ during the final three and one half years of the Great Tribulation (Rev. 14:13). They will then be given a glorified body and will reign with Christ for one thousand years. We note that this is the final chapter for the first resurrection which commenced with Jesus Christ, the "first fruits," at Calvary almost two thousand years ago.
4. **The Judgment of the Nations:** Also known as the Sheep and Goat Judgment as detailed in Matthew 25:31-46.
   - ■ *The unsaved* go to eternal judgment--at the Great White Throne.
   - ■ *The saved* (those without the mark of the Beast) will enter the Millennial Kingdom in their fleshly bodies to repopulate the earth under the reign of a theocracy--Jesus Christ.

Conditions on Earth During the Millennium?

1. **Israel Will Be Established In a "Garden of Eden"**-- occupying all that land from the river of Egypt to the Euphrates River. *"In the same day the Lord made a covenant with Abram, saying, Unto thy seed have I given this land, from the river of Egypt unto the great river, the river Euphrates"* (Gen. 15:18). *"Thou hast increased the*

nation, O Lord, thou hast increased the nation: thou art glorified: thou hadst removed it far unto all the ends of the earth'' (Isa. 26:15).

2. **The Physical Scene:**
   a. **Land features will change.** *"And it shall come to pass in the last days, that the mountain of the Lord's house shall be established in the top of the mountains, and shall be exalted above the hills; and all nations shall flow unto it''* (Isa. 2:2). *"And it shall come to pass, that the fishers shall stand upon it from Engedi even unto Eneglaim; they shall be a place to spread forth nets; their fish shall be according to their kinds, as the fish of the great sea, exceeding many''* (Ezek. 47:10). *"And his feet shall stand in that day upon the mount of Olives, which is before Jerusalem on the east, and the mount of Olives shall cleave in the midst thereof toward the east and toward the west, and there shall be a very great valley; and half of the mountain shall remove toward the north, and half of it toward the south''* (Zech. 14:4).
   b. **Jerusalem will have an independent source of water.** *"And it shall come to pass in that day, that the mountains shall drop down new wine, and the hills shall flow with milk, and all the rivers of Judah shall flow with waters, and a fountain shall come forth out of the house of the Lord, and shall water the valley of Shittim''* (Joel 3:18).
   c. **Abundance of grain, good, and wine in Israel.** *"And the floors shall be full of wheat, and the vats shall overflow with wine and oil. And I will restore to you the years that the locust hath eaten, the cankerworm, and the caterpillar, and the palmerworm, my great army which I sent among you. And ye shall eat in plenty, and be satisfied, and praise the name of the Lord your God, that hath dealt wondrously with you: and my people shall never be ashamed. And ye shall know that I am in the midst of Israel, and that I am the Lord your God, and none else:*

and my people shall never be ashamed'' (Joel 2:24-27). *''And I will raise up for them a plant of renown, and they shall be no more consumed with hunger in the land, neither bear the shame of the heathen any more''* (Ezek. 34:29). *''Behold, the days come, saith the Lord, that the plowman shall overtake the reaper, and the treader of grapes him that soweth seed; and the mountains shall drop sweet wine, and all the hills shall melt''* (Amos 9:13).

3. **Weather Conditions:** Today the land is noted for its harsh climatic conditions, but in the Millennium rain will come at the appointed time. *''Be glad then, ye children of Zion, and rejoice in the Lord your God: for he hath given you the former rain moderately, and he will cause to come down for you the rain, the former rain, and the latter rain in the first month''* (Joel 2: 23). *''And I will make them and the places round about my hill a blessing; and I will cause the shower to come down in his season; there shall be showers of blessing. And the tree of the field shall yield her fruit, and the earth shall yield her increase, and they shall be safe in their land, and shall know that I am the Lord, when I have broken the bands of their yoke, and delivered them out of the hand of those that served themselves of them''* (Ezek. 34:26-27).

4. **Security of Tenure:** The Jews will be in their land for the entire period of Christ's reign, never again to be evicted. *''And it shall come to pass in that day, that the Lord shall set his hand again the second time to recover the remnant of his people. . . . And he shall set up an ensign for the nations, and shall assemble the outcasts of Israel, and gather together the dispersed of Judah from the four corners of the earth''* (Isa. 11:11-12). *''And I will bring again the captivity of my people of Israel, and they shall build the waste cities, and inhabit them; and they shall plant vineyards, and drink the wine thereof; they shall also*

make gardens, and eat the fruit of them. And I will plant them upon their land, and they shall no more be pulled up out of their land which I have given them, saith the Lord thy God'' (Amos 9:14-15). *''So shall ye divide this land unto you according to the tribes of Israel. And it shall come to pass, that ye shall divide it by lot for an inheritance unto you, and to the strangers that sojourn among you, which shall beget children among you: and they shall be unto you as born in the country among the children of Israel; they shall have inheritance with you among the tribes of Israel''* (Ezek. 47:21-22).

5. **No More Evil:** It will be a land characterized by peace, justice, and righteousness. *''For unto us a child is born, unto us a son is given: and the government shall be upon his shoulder: and his name shall be called Wonderful, Counsellor, The mighty God, The everlasting Father, The Prince of Peace. Of the increase of his government and peace there shall be no end, upon the throne of David, and upon his kingdom, to order it, and to establish it with judgment and with justice from henceforth even for ever. The zeal of the Lord of hosts will perform this''* (Isa. 9:6-7). *''And he shall judge among many people, and rebuke strong nations afar off; and they shall beat their swords into plowshares, and their spears into pruninghooks: nation shall not lift up a sword against nation, neither shall they learn war any more''* (Mic. 4:3). *''But unto the Son he saith, Thy throne, O God, is for ever and ever: a sceptre of righteousness is the sceptre of thy kingdom''* (Heb. 1:8).

6. **The Environment Will Be Normal.** *''And the inhabitant shall not say, I am sick: the people that dwell therein shall be forgiven their iniquity''* (Isa. 33:24). *''Then the eyes of the blind shall be opened, and the ears of the deaf shall be unstopped. Then shall the lame man leap as an hart, and the tongue of the dumb sing: for in the wilderness shall waters break out, and streams in the desert. And the*

parched ground shall become a pool, and the thirsty land springs of water: in the habitation of dragons, where each lay, shall be grass with reeds and rushes'' (Isa. 35:5-7). *''For, behold, I create new heavens and a new earth: and the former shall not be remembered, nor come into mind. But be ye glad and rejoice for ever in that which I create: for, behold, I create Jerusalem a rejoicing, and her people a joy. And I will rejoice in Jerusalem, and joy in my people: and the voice of weeping shall be no more heard in her, nor the voice of crying. There shall be no more thence an infant of days, nor an old man that hath not filled his days: for the child shall die an hundred years old; but the sinner being an hundred years old shall be accursed. And they shall build houses, and inhabit them; and they shall plant vineyards, and eat the fruit of them. They shall not build, and another inhabit; they shall not plant, and another eat: for as the days of a tree are the days of my people, and mine elect shall long enjoy the work of their hands. They shall not labour in vain, nor bring forth for trouble; for they are the seed of the blessed of the Lord, and their offspring with them. And it shall come to pass, that before they call, I will answer; and while they are yet speaking, I will hear. The wolf and the lamb shall feed together, and the lion shall eat straw like the bullock: and dust shall be the serpent's meat. They shall not hurt nor destroy in all my holy mountain, saith the Lord''* (Isa. 65:17-25).

Conclusion

The conditions just outlined are those for Israel during the Millennium. The question we must now ask is this: What will it be like for the rest of the world? The Word of God leaves us in no doubt.

*''They shall not hurt nor destroy in all my holy mountain: for the **earth** shall be full of the*

knowledge of the Lord, as the waters cover the sea'' (Isa. 11:9).

*''He shall have dominion also from sea to sea, and from the river unto the **ends of the earth** ''* (Ps. 72:8).

*''And he shall judge among the **nations**, and shall rebuke many people: and they shall beat their swords into plowshares, and their spears into pruninghooks: **nation** shall not lift up sword against nation, neither shall they learn war any more''* (Isa. 2:4).

It is appropriate to conclude this chapter with the glorious words from our blessed Master and coming Redeemer--words of hope for a troubled society and degenerate generation:

''And I heard as it were the voice of a great multitude, and as the voice of many waters, and as the voice of mighty thunderings, saying, Alleluia: for the Lord God omnipotent reigneth'' (Rev. 19:6).

''And the Spirit and the bride say, Come. And let him that heareth say, Come. And let him that is athirst come. And whosoever will, let him take the water of life freely. . . . He which testifieth these things saith, Surely I come quickly. Amen. Even so, come, Lord Jesus'' (Rev. 22:17,20).

Even so, come, Lord Jesus. Amen.

Characteristics and Nature of the Millennium

1. **Peace**--Isaiah 2:4; 11:6-9; 65:21; Hosea 2:18; Micah 4:2-5; Zechariah 9:10
2. **Joy**--Isaiah 9:3; 30:19,29; 65:18; Zephaniah 3:14-17
3. **Holiness**--Isaiah 1:26-27; 35:8-10; Zephaniah 3:11
4. **Glory**--Isaiah 4:2; 40:3-5
5. **Comfort**--Isaiah 12:1-2; 40:1; Jeremiah 31:23-25
6. **Justice**--Isaiah 9:6-7 (Jer. 30:9; Ezek. 34:23; Hos. 3:5); Isaiah 32:16
7. **Computer Knowledge**--Isaiah 11:9; 54:13; Habakkuk 2:14
8. **Instruction**--Isaiah 2:2-3 (Mic. 4:1-3); Jeremiah 3:14-15
9. **Removal of the Curse**--Isaiah 11:6-9; 65:25
10. **Sickness Removed**--Isaiah 33:24; 35:5-7; Zephaniah 3:19
11. **Freedom from Oppression**--Isaiah 14:3-7; Amos 9:15; Zechariah 9:8; 14:10-11
12. **Longevity Will Be Restored**--Isaiah 65:20
13. **Reproduction by Human Saints**--Isaiah 65:35; Ezekiel 47:21-22; Zechariah 10:8
14. **Labor**--Isaiah 62:8-9; 65:21-23; Ezekiel 48:18-19
15. **Economic Prosperity**--Isaiah 30:23-25; 35:1-2,7; Amos 9:13-15; Joel 2:21-27
16. **Increase in Light**--Isaiah 4:5-6; 30:26; 60:19-20; Zechariah 2:5
17. **Unified Language**--Zephaniah 3:9
18. **Unified Worship**--Isaiah 52:1,7-10; Malachi 1:11; Zechariah 8:23; 14:16
19. **Manifest Presence of God**--Ezekiel 37:26-28; Zechariah 2:10-13
20. **Palestine Will Be Enlarged**--Isaiah 26:15; Obadiah 1:17-21; Genesis 15:18
21. **Land Features Will Change**--Zechariah 14:4,8,10; Isaiah 2:2; Ezekiel 47:8-12
22. **Jerusalem Will Become the Worship Center of the World**--Micah 4:1

23. **Jerusalem Renamed**--Will be 9.6 kilometers in circumference--Ezekiel 48:35
24. **It Will Have a Temple**--Isaiah 2:3; Ezekiel 40-48; Joel 3:18; Haggai 2:7-9

Notes

1. Churchill, Sir Winston. *His Complete Speeches*, edited by Robert R. James, Volume vii, p. 7488.
2. *Time*, International Edition, December 31, 1990.
3. *Der Speigel*, September 13, 1993. Reprinted in *Strait Sunday Times*, September 19, 1993.
4. *The Australian*, May 8, 1992.
5. *Maranatha Prophetic Alert*, No. 89, March 1993. World news report by Don E. Stanton.
6. Marrs, Texe, *Flashpoint*, February 1993.

Chapter 5

The Antichrist System: Government and Religion

Dr. Robert Lindsted

Maybe you think you are informed about the New Age movement, but the inroads made by New Agers are so subtle and so cunning that I believe unless you are constantly on guard, the subtle lie of Satan that took its toll in the Garden of Eden will also take its toll on you. There is a saying, *"Those that stand for nothing will fall for anything."* Today we have the idea that as long as we ignore the New Age movement, it's never going to attack our home or our children. Nothing can be further from the truth. We need to stay aware and stand on the Word of God to defend ourselves from this lie of Satan called the New Age.

I want to share with you the basic viewpoints of the New Age and look at some areas where I see the New Age making incredible inroads into our lives.

Why is it so important for us to know about the New Age? For one thing, the Bible is very clear that in the last days there will be an end-time religion. Notice that I said "religion" . . . not Christianity. I believe that the enemy of Christianity is religion. Think about it. Who were the people who crucified Christ? They were religious men, weren't they? People have the idea that one religion is like another, but nothing could be further from the truth. The most religious people I know live in India. They won't eat hamburger because it might be a relative. Those are religious people. I'm not religious. I'm a Christian. There is a lot of difference.

I think Satan would rather have a person be religious than any other way. His trophy is not the drunk in the gutter or the drug addict. His trophies are religious, "good" people who may tithe regularly, have Sunday school papers in their pockets, and even carry a Bible from time to time. But if they've never had a personal relationship with Jesus Christ, they're not saved. The New Age is aimed directly at those people.

The Bible says that the last religious system will be worldwide. It will be religion at its best. It will be Christianity's enemy. If we're honest with ourselves and look at the situation around us in the world today and compare it to what the Bible says, we can see this last religious system. The Bible identifies it as a worldwide uniting force. The Bible also talks about a lost political system, the New World Order, that will join hands with the religious system and economic system that will be at its greatest hour and then collapse overnight.

2 Timothy 3:1-2 says:

"This know also, that in the last days perilous times shall come. For men shall be lovers of their own selves. . . ."

This is the key. This new religion called the New Age specializes in the so-called self-esteem religion. It proclaims the idea that we are gods. Whenever they talk about a person being a god, it's always capitalized G-O-D. But whenever they talk about God the Father or God the Creator, it is always lowercase, g-o-d. I think that is quite a pronouncement, don't you? The Bible says, "Here's how you'll know. In the last days men will be lovers of their own self." The sign, the indicator of the last days is a false religion where people actually believe in themselves more than they believe in God.

Matthew 24 is another great prophetic chapter. It concerns the time of the Tribulation period.

> *"And Jesus answered and said unto them* [the twelve apostles], *Take heed that no man deceive you. For many shall come in my name, saying, I am Christ; and shall deceive many . . . And many false prophets shall rise, and shall deceive many . . . For there shall arise false Christs, and false prophets, and shall shew great signs and wonders; insomuch that, if it were possible* [thank God, it's not!], *they shall deceive the very elect"* (Matt. 24:4-5,11,24).

Now, that's a powerful deception, isn't it? It says that people who ought to know better when they see the great lie that Satan has prepared will actually believe it. That's certainly what happened in the Garden of Eden.

Now, don't get the idea that Eve was some backward, naive girl. I think Eve was a thinking woman. I think she had great reasoning power, but Satan challenged her. He said to her, "Do you mean that you can eat of almost every tree in this garden, but He won't let you eat the fruit of that one? Come on, what's wrong with the fruit? Name something wrong with that fruit." Now, she's a thinking woman and says, "You're right. After all, if we can eat of any other tree, what would be wrong with this one?" The problem was she disobeyed God.

Genesis 3 says,

> *"Now the serpent was more subtil than any beast of the field which the Lord God had made. And he said unto the woman, Yea, hath God said, Ye shall not eat of every tree of the*

garden? And the woman said unto the serpent,
We may eat of the fruit of the trees of the
garden: But of the fruit of the tree which is in
the midst of the garden, God hath said, Ye shall
not eat of it, neither shall ye touch it, lest ye
die'' (Gen. 3:1-3).

It's important for us to realize in this exchange of words
between the serpent and Eve there are three lies that are told.
In one lie, Satan simply leaves out one word of truth. For
another lie he simply adds one extra word, and in the other lie
he changes the order of the words. That's not much. What's
one word? Let me give you an example with these two
sentences with only one word difference. ''She is very pretty.''
''She is not very pretty.'' Does one word change anything?
Sure it does. But all Satan said was, ''you shall not surely die.''
Eve said, ''If we eat of this tree, we'll die,'' and the serpent said,
''You shall not.'' All he did was add the word ''not.''

> *''. . . Ye shall not surely die. For God doth know*
> *that in the day ye eat thereof, then your eyes*
> *shall be opened, and ye shall be as gods,*
> *knowing good and evil''* (Gen. 3:4-5).

That's a very clear statement of what the subtle lie was.
Satan told Eve, ''God doesn't want you to become as great as
He is, so He doesn't want you to know good and evil. He's
trying to limit you.'' Satan convinced Eve that if she disobeyed,
she would become God. That was his promise to her. But what
happened? All she did was prove that she was a sinner. She
proved that she was not God.

> *''Because that, when they knew God, they*
> *glorified him not as God, neither were thank-*
> *ful; but became vain in their imaginations, and*

their foolish heart was darkened. Professing themselves to be wise, they became fools, And changed the glory of the uncorruptible God into an image made like to corruptible man, and to birds, and fourfooted beasts, and creeping things . . . Who changed the truth of God into a lie . . . '' (Rom. 1:21-23,25).

The downfall was that these people actually began to worship the thing that was created, including man, more than the Creator who was God. They exchanged the truth of God for a lie. The lie is this . . . that you and I are gods. That's the message of the New Age. I think that the worst enemy of the Christian might be ignorance. I really believe that those who stand for nothing will fall for anything. As we look around at the bombardment of the New Age, we find that we can see how it is encroaching on our thinking and our lives. People take up yoga, get involved in holistic health, read books on Eastern religions, search for a guru, lobby for meditation in public schools, or write books about it. These are all part of the practices that people seem to think can bring great benefit to humanity. The New Age sees humanity poised on the edge of a worldwide transformation. The supporters believe that the world's economic, military, social, and political problems can be solved by releasing human potential.

The essential idea behind the New Age consciousness is that all is one. It emphasizes that man is one with Mother Earth. It denies any separation between humans and nature, between humans and God, and says the universe is a seamless garment, a perfect unity. In other words, there is no difference between a dog, a cat, a wooden table, and me. I don't know about you, and I probably haven't gone as far in the sciences as I should, but I think there are some basic differences between a chunk of wood and a human. But New Age people are not very scientific and if they can say there is no difference between a table and a dog, and there is no difference between a dog and a human, then they can go on to say, "There is no difference between a human and God."

Another of their basic ideas is that "all is God." The Christian view of a personal God is abandoned in favor of an impersonal energy force or consciousness. It is the Eastern religions, such as Hinduism or Buddhism. The New Age god is more an 'it' than a person. It's the "force" of *Star Wars.*

New Age thinking claims that we are all gods whether we realize it or not. The thinking goes something like this: The God of the Bible is dethroned; humans are crowned supreme. The Father in Heaven is replaced by the divine within every one of us.

I think this is a lie, and I think that lie comes from the pit of hell. I don't believe this is the basic building block that will bring all humanity to peace. I think it's the basic building block that will bring all humanity under the captivation of the Antichrist. By the grace of God he'll never be able to complete his devilish work until the church is gone.

How do you have a New Age experience? Here's what they say: "You can attain a New Age experience through drugs, through meditation, through Eastern meditation, through yoga, through martial arts, through hypnosis, through biofeedback, through sex. When you have sex, you are exercising your right as a god, so it's not wrong. There is no such thing as sin and guilt."

You can imagine why this is the fastest growing religion on college campuses today. There are simply no rules. You say, "That's fine. That's theory, but how does that translate into things that are practical?" Let me try to show you. Let's take, just for example, the aspect of advertisement. Lest you think I'm making this up, I will quote from the *New York Times.* This is not a Christian publication. It talks about the New Age, and it begins to list all kinds of New Age ads. Here's what they say:

*"Representatives of some of the nation's larg-
est corporations, including IBM, AT&T, and
General Motors, met in New Mexico to discuss
how metaphysics, the occult, and Hindu mysticism can help executives compete in the
marketplace.*

   *"They are honest about who's involved.
On one level they say: 'It is evidenced by the
surge of interest in new metaphysic religions,
mediums, the occult, reincarnations, psychic
healings, Satanism, spirit guides, and other
aspects of supernatural phenomena and belief.' On another level, the scholars cite the
spreading influence of the psychological self-
help in human potential groups. On both levels, leaders contend they are ushering in what
they call a New Age of understanding in intellectual fervor as significant as the Renaissance. What is changing, researchers say, is
that an increasing number of middle-class
Americans, many of them middle-aged, are
showing an interest in supernatural phenomena that blend Eastern mystic and Western
occult thinking. I think it is as much a political
movement as a religious movement. It is spreading into business management theory and a lot
of other areas. If you look at it closely, you see
it represents a complete rejection of Judeo-
Christian and bedrock American values."*

Now that's their summary. This guy is not even a
believer. It goes on to say:

*"Most would argue that mankind is on a
threshold, a great evolutionary leap of con-*

sciousness. How did it begin? It was introduced to us on a large scale by a force in George Lucas' Star Wars films. It made its way through entertainment and advertisement; now, despite such criticism, the New Age has found its way into the Stanford University's well-regarded Graduate School of Business. Now, Harvard has courses on the New Age.''

And so on and so on, and they list the whole process. In an article out of a magazine called *Insight*, it says:

''For most Americans the New Age is a harmless mix of Shirley MacLaine, channelers, and crystals, but for a smaller number of Christians around the United States, the spiritual and psychological beliefs that characterize the New Age movement are nothing less than the work of Satan.''

I want you to know that I don't mind being in the minority. I'm one of those people who think the New Age is the work of Satan. Here is a summary of the seven important doctrinal points of view for the New Age.

1. *''Jesus was not and is not the only Christ, nor is He God.''* Now, this is incredible! They are also going to tell you that every one of us is gods, but the only one who isn't God is Jesus. Does that make any sense? The only one who really deserves to be called God is the Lord Jesus Christ, but they say, ''No, you are god.'' But then they say Jesus was not and is not God.

2. *''God is impersonal, cosmic, a God of*

energy forces. He's not a person. He's kind of a wind that blows; a feeling that you have.'' A hot, sticky feeling. That's just a popsicle that melted on a hot, summer night.

3. *''Man is himself god for he consists of and is the creator of the forces. Man already exercises the power inherent in his divinity and needs only to awaken to this fact.''* In other words, look at that child you have, the one that's giving you so much trouble. If you could just show him that he's god then everything will be all right. Do you see that this message is exactly the opposite of what the Bible says? You know what the Bible says you are? A sinner. The Bible says the wages of sin is death. The New Age says, ''No, you are gods.'' The trouble is this godness is buried in you and you have to ''discover'' it, you have to ''wake up'' the god that is in you.

4. *''Man should seek and accept spiritual instruction and direction directly from the spirit world.''* The state of Kansas education system actually says our children need spiritual teachers. For example, to help you do algebra, you need a spirit guide. I can show you this in our public schools. The New Age says, ''That's right. You need to accept spiritual instruction directly from the spirit world.''

5. *''All religions and religious teachings lead to the same goal. All have equal merit.''* Now what does the Bible say? In the Bible Christ says, *''I am the way, the truth, and the life.''* The Bible says we are exclusive.

The New Age says it doesn't matter if we are Hindu, Buddhist, Catholic, Protestant; we are all on the road going to the same place. Robert Shuller says that *"It doesn't matter what you believe. Easter . . . it's these flowers, it's red flowers, it's yellow flowers, green flowers, and blue flowers. It doesn't matter."* In his message to the Russian people, he said, *"Believe in God, who believes in you. Maybe our ideologies are different, but it doesn't matter. We're all children of God."* I tell you what, Robert Shuller has no idea of what it means to be a child of God if he thinks we're all the children of God. Finally, if you can find a god who believes in you, then don't believe in him because he's not God. Think about it. If whoever you think is God believes in you, then he's not God because you can't be trusted. You know what? You are a sinner. The Bible is the one who exposes us to what sin is.

6. *"The ancient wisdom of Babylon, Egypt, and Greece, not the Bible, is the basis of all truth."* Isn't it interesting that they would use Babylon. In Revelation 17 and 18 it talks about the mystery harlot of Babylon. I don't know what this does to your blood pressure, but I know what it does to mine.

7. *"Sin and evil do not exist. Peace and love are the ultimate realities."* Those are the seven basic principles of the New Age.

The New World Order In Bible Prophecy

When President Bush made his first speech concerning

the Gulf War at the National Religious Broadcasters Convention in Washington, D.C., to an audience of about four thousand, the president presented his stand on the war, and then went on to say,

> *"You know what is going to solve all of our problems? There is something new called the New World Order. When this comes in, it's going to bring peace as we have never seen. We are going to be able to lay down all of our weapons. The New World Order is the solution to all of our problems."*

Most of the several thousand religious broadcasters stood and applauded the president. Only a dozen or so people remained seated. Stunned, they wondered, as I did, "Can this really be happening?"

Many who heard that speech did not realize the significance of the president's words. But those of us who have studied biblical prophecy knew George Bush was articulating in a public forum what we knew would come to pass someday.

The New World Order will indeed bring the world together under one government, but it will create more problems than it will solve. In fact, in the end this New World Order will neatly give its power to the Antichrist exactly as the Bible predicted hundreds of years ago.

What is an antichrist? It is one who will pretend to be everything for which Christ stands, but he will be the exact opposite. So, he is anti-christ because he is really opposed to Christ. He will pretend he is the Christ, hoping to win the affection of people.

The Bible says there will come a time when there will be one world government with one economic system under the control of one man. Scripture says there will be a revived Roman Empire that will rule for a short time. Then, people will give their allegiance to this Antichrist for the rest of time.

These predictions were given to the prophet Daniel some twenty-five hundred years ago; and to the Apostle John some nineteen hundred years ago. Bible prophecy is different from the predictions found at the grocery tabloid counter-- those predictions were made last week with most of them never coming true. The Bible's predictions were made hundreds of years ago, and every one of them will come true; not some, but all of them!

The Royal Nightmare

One night, about twenty-five hundred years ago, King Nebuchadnezzar had a nightmare. After tossing and turning, he sat up in bed and said, "I have just had this royal dream, and I know it is important because if I dreamed it, it has to be important. Nothing but important things go through my mind."

He called for the royal wise men and demanded they tell him the royal interpretation of his royal dream. "If you will tell us the royal dream, Your Highness, we will make up the royal lie; we mean the royal interpretation," they replied. The king interrupted them. "As a matter of fact, I've been meaning to talk to you about that. I tell you my dreams, and you guys make up these interpretations that never come true. If you are so smart, you figure out what I dreamed and then the meaning of it, too!" "Oh, no!" they quickly reminded him. "That's not in our royal contract."

The king responded, "I tell you what. If you can't figure out the dream and give me its interpretation, I am going to cut off your heads." (This threat was extended to the prophet Daniel, too.) Now, Daniel was a Hebrew, who, as a teenager, had been taken from his home in Jerusalem and transported some eight hundred miles away to the conquering Babylonians. When he was brought to this foreign kingdom, they tried to change his name, his language, and his diet. He said, "Wait a minute! You will have to excuse me, but you see,

I'm a Jewish boy. There are certain things a Jewish boy doesn't eat or drink. If you don't mind, I'll have my own food, and I will eat that instead.'' ''Oh, Daniel,'' the king urged, ''when in Babylon, do as the Babylonians do.'' But Daniel refused that generous invitation. Since Daniel was not afraid to take a stand, God blessed him. God is still looking for young people who will take a stand. If they do, He will bless them. God delights in blessing people.

When Daniel heard about the execution notice, he went to King Nebuchadnezzar and said, ''Would it be okay, before you chop our heads off, if I pray to my God?'' The king answered, ''Sure, you can pray.'' Daniel had more freedom to pray in a foreign language than we do in our public schools today! Isn't that pathetic? But, it is true.

The Head of Gold

Daniel prayed, and God told him the king's dream and its interpretation! The next day, Daniel went back into the king's presence and said, ''Listen, king, I think I know what you saw in your vision. You saw a huge image with its top made of gold.'' Amazed, the king admitted that was his dream. ''How did you know?'' he asked. Daniel replied that his God had revealed the dream to him and went on to tell the king the rest of the dream.

''After the head of gold, there was a chest and arms of silver. The belly and thighs were of bronze with legs of iron. The feet were part iron and part clay. They were extensions of the legs, but clay had been mingled with the iron.'' The king was in astonishment, ''That is exactly what I saw!''

Daniel continued with the dream. ''You then saw a stone that looked as if it came out of the mountain, but it was not cut with hands. As it came, it rolled toward the image and crushed it. In fact, it ground the image into powder. The stone then began to grow until it filled the entire earth.'' The bewildered king then said, ''That's exactly what I saw! But, what does it mean?''

Daniel said, ''All right, here is the interpretation, and it is a sure one. If my God could show me the dream, then His interpretation of it is sure.'' He then said, *''Thou, O King, art the head of gold.''* Nebuchadnezzar liked this interpretation. Frankly, I don't think he heard another word Daniel said. I believe he thought, Wow! I am the head of gold...that's me. That's me, all right, way up there on the top!

What did he do? He built a golden image to himself and placed it in the plain of Shinar. As everyone came from all over the world, they would bow down to the golden image of him. Yes, he liked that interpretation.

Daniel, however, told him, ''God said you are not going to be the king forever. You are going to be replaced by another country that is inferior to you. It will be the silver. After it will come another, even more inferior nation, and it will take over the world. It will be the bronze. Then, there will be another part with two legs of iron that will be yet another kingdom. Finally, at the end of time, there will be ten toes. They are part iron and part clay; and they are going to be an extension of those iron legs, even though they will be another kingdom. However, this kingdom will rule only a little while. A stone will come and crush all of it. This stone will begin a kingdom of which there will be no end.''

This stone is none other than the Kingdom of God. Remember, when Christ begins to rule and reign, He will rule forever.

The Ram and the Goat

Let's look at Daniel's prophecies concerning the two world empires that were to follow King Nebuchadnezzar's Babylonian Empire:

> *''And after thee shall arise another kingdom inferior to thee, and another third kingdom of*

brass, which shall bear rule over all the earth''
(Dan. 2:39).

These kingdoms have come into reality, exactly as the Bible said. In the book of Daniel, not one time but four times, God described every world power, in order, and called them by name. In order to understand their significance, look at what Daniel 8:3-8 says:

''Then I lifted up mine eyes, and saw, and, behold, there stood before the river a ram which had two horns: and the two horns were high; but one was higher than the other, and the higher came up last. I saw the ram pushing westward, and northward, and southward; so that no beasts might stand before him, neither was there any that could deliver out of his hand; but he did according to his will, and became great. And as I was considering, behold, an he goat came from the west on the face of the whole earth, and touched not the ground: and the goat had a notable horn between his eyes. And he came to the ram that had two horns, which I had seen standing before the river, and ran unto him in the fury of his power. And I saw him come close unto the ram, and he was moved with choler against him, and smote the ram, and brake his two horns: and there was no power in the ram to stand before him, but he cast him down to the ground, and stamped upon him: and there was none that could deliver the ram out of his hand. Therefore the he goat waxed very great: and when he was strong, the great horn was broken; and for it came up four notable ones toward the four

winds of heaven.''

After the head of gold, which was Nebuchadnezzar's Babylon, the kingdom of the Medes and the Persians became the next world power. The two arms represent the two parts of their kingdom. In verse 20 Daniel writes, *''The ram which thou sawest having two horns are the kings of Media and Persia.''* Like a lopsided ram with one horn bigger than the other, the Persian Empire would come up last and be the dominant power. Just as Daniel predicted, that is exactly what happened.

The third kingdom, represented in this vision as the mean he-goat with one horn who beat up the ram with two horns, began to rule the world. This is the Grecian Empire seen as the belly and thighs of bronze in the king's dream. Then, when the he-goat was in his prime--in his great fury--the big horn broke, and four horns popped out of his head. The kingdom represented by the he-goat was that of Alexander the Great, the dominant king of Greece who died in his prime. His four generals took power after him. Look at verse 21: *''And the rough goat is the king of Grecia: and the great horn that is between his eyes is the first king.''* Isn't that pretty simple? That is Alexander the Great.

Alexander the Great conquered the world when he was barely thirty years old, and then became frustrated because there was nothing else to conquer. Instead, he went around the world putting on marching exhibitions. He caught a marsh fever and died a fool's death while putting on a parade. His generals came home to his infant son to say, ''Your daddy's dead, now you rule the world.'' The son asked, ''What do I do with the world?'' It is recorded that the four generals of Alexander the Great killed his son and divided the kingdom among themselves.

Consider what the Bible said one hundred and seventy-five years before Alexander the Great was ever born! Verses 21 and 22 state: *''. . . and the great horn that is between his eyes is the first king. Now that being broken, whereas four stood up for it, four kingdoms shall stand up out of the nation, but not in his power.''* These verses refer to Alexander the Great, and the last verse tells us that his son would not rule after him. Isn't the Bible clear? The head of gold is Babylon; the arms and chest of silver are the Medes and the Persians; and the belly and thighs of bronze are none other than Alexander the Great.

These empires are recorded in yet another manner. Daniel described them as three animals: the first one, like a lion with eagle's wings (Babylon); next, a bear with three ribs in his mouth (the Medo-Persians--this is a matter of recorded history); and third, a leopard with four wings that depict the swiftness of Alexander the Great's world conquest.

The Fourth Kingdom

What about the fourth kingdom? In the interpretation of the king's dream, Daniel wrote:

> *"And the fourth kingdom shall be strong as iron: forasmuch as iron breaketh in pieces and subdueth all things: and as iron that breaketh all these, shall it break in pieces and bruise. And whereas thou sawest the feet and toes, part of potters' clay, and part of iron, the kingdom shall be divided; but there shall be in it of the strength of the iron, forasmuch as thou sawest the iron mixed with miry clay. And as the toes of the feet were part of iron, and part of clay, so the kingdom shall be partly strong, and partly broken. And whereas thou sawest iron mixed with miry clay, they shall mingle themselves with the seed of men: but they shall not cleave one to another, even as iron is not mixed with clay. And in the days of these kings shall the God of heaven set up a kingdom, which*

shall never be destroyed: and the kingdom shall not be left to other people, but it shall break in pieces and consume all these kingdoms, and it shall stand for ever. Forasmuch as thou sawest that the stone was cut out of the mountain without hands, and that it brake in pieces the iron, the brass, the clay, the silver, and the gold; the great God hath made known to the king what shall come to pass hereafter: and the dream is certain, and the interpretation thereof sure'' (Dan. 2:40-45).

What kingdom do the legs of iron represent? The Roman Empire with its two capitals: Rome and Constantinople. How do we know? Revelation 17:10 tells us that seven kings will rule the world. The first two were Assyria and Egypt. Then Daniel comes in chronologically with Babylon as number three. The fourth and fifth kingdoms were the Medes and the Persians, followed by Alexander the Great. In verses 10-13 we find:

''And there are seven kings: five are fallen, and one is, and the other is not yet come; and when he cometh, he must continue a short space. And the beast that was, and is not, even he is the eighth, and is of the seven, and goeth into perdition. And the ten horns which thou sawest are ten kings, which have received no kingdom as yet; but receive power as kings one hour with the beast. These have one mind, and shall give their power and strength unto the beast.''

The Bible says, *''five are fallen, one is.''* Who would be in power when Revelation was written at about A.D. 95 or A.D.

96?--Rome. This passage states there are seven kings; five are fallen, one is right now, and the other will come later. The last kingdom will be an extension of the iron legs that Daniel wrote about. It will be a revived Roman Empire. It will be part iron and part clay, a mixture of religion and politics. In Daniel 7:7-8 we read:

> *"After this I saw in the night visions, and behold a fourth beast, dreadful and terrible, and strong exceedingly; and it had great iron teeth: it devoured and brake in pieces, and stamped the residue with the feet of it: and it was diverse from all the beasts that were before it; and it had ten horns. I considered the horns, and, behold, there came up among them another little horn, before whom there were three of the first horns plucked up by the roots: and, behold, in this horn were eyes like the eyes of man, and a mouth speaking great things."*

In verse 7, Daniel said he saw a beast so terrible, it was like nothing he had ever seen before. This dreadful, ugly beast was so strong that it had great iron teeth (like the iron legs). It broke all the other kingdoms. Ten horns then came up representing ten kings--in other words, an extension of those legs would be the feet, part of iron and part of clay.

The Revived Roman Empire

The Bible states what has and is going to happen. There will be Babylon; the Medes and the Persians; Greece and Alexander the Great; the Roman Empire; and then an extension of one--a revived Roman Empire with ten horns or ten kings. Once this last kingdom comes to power, it will rule for one hour, and then will give its power to the Beast. He will rule and make war against the Lamb.

An article in the *Wichita Eagle* stated,

> "*. . . Since the fall of the Roman Empire, there has been the dream of a unified Europe. We are . . . seeing a brand new Roman Empire reconstructed.*"

Even news reporters call the unified Europe the new Roman Empire. On December 31, 1992, the European Economic Community took power, and on January 1, 1993, its policies went into effect. Until recently, the European Community was considered to be only a political coalition. Now, it has gone from an economic dream to a political reality.

The *Kansas City Star* recently ran an article, "Is Euro-Man Kinda' Like Superman?" It goes on to state that most of western Europe will be combined into one big, powerful, economic unit that will be the envy of the world. Will it work? Will it dominate America? Will America be second class? The answer is yes. The European Community is on the verge of becoming the dominant power of the world. It is a revived Roman Empire. *Northwest Magazine*, sponsored by an airline, carried an article declaring that America will take a back seat to the revived Roman Empire.

After the Persian Gulf Crisis, I flew back from Israel and landed in Greece. I was handed a card stating that any person who is a citizen of any one of the twelve Common Market nations would not have to fill out any legal papers when going from one country to another in Europe. However, any person who is not from one of the Common Market nations would have to fill out all of the papers.

Forbes magazine wrote: "*There will only be one Europe. It will be a super power.*" Will there be one currency, or many? This magazine answers:

> "*Ultimately, the move to a single currency is*

*about symbolism and power. There will be only
one economy, and it will not only be a united
Europe, but it will probably be a united world.''*

In the business section of the previously quoted European newspaper, there is a very interesting second section depicting what Europeans describe as a historical moment--''Making History, A Unique Moment As World Leaders Gather In London.'' Why? To launch the first test for the Euro-bank and the new Euro-dollar. It's already here; it's already been issued; and now, it's on its way.

The New World Order

How close are we to the New World Order? An article in the *Atlantic Journal* begins by announcing a New World Order--a world quite different from the one we have known--with a United Nations that performs as envisioned by its founders. It goes on to say that following the Persian Gulf Crisis, the New World Order is emerging as our only hope for peace around the world. This is it. Utopia. It is finally here, bringing the nations of the world under one government. If we have one government, we will have no wars, they say. This deceptive promise of heaven on earth is winning great popularity. Howard Wilkins, an ambassador to one of the Common Market nations said,

*"We will not recognize the world because of
the change militarily and politically in Europe. Once it is united, it will be as big or
bigger than the United States in terms of its
marketing power.''*

He is right. Soon we may not recognize the world. The truthful observer must agree that America is in decay. A new superstar is on the scene--a united Europe--a revived Roman

Empire exactly as the Bible said. The Common Market says to the industrialized nations, "Hey, the United States is in decline. If you want to look at the future, you'd better align with the Common Market--the seat of world power."

Presently, there are twelve countries in the Common Market with several others who want in. Do you know what is so interesting about that? The Bible states that when the Antichrist comes to power, he will pull three nations out. Then he will put himself in power, allowing only ten nations to remain. Now, if he is going to pull out three and leave ten, that means he will have begun with thirteen. In a special edition of the *Jerusalem Post*, which featured the twelve stars of the Common Market nations, guess which nation the *Post* was recommending for number thirteen? The Israeli Star of David! Entering Europe's charmed circle seems to be Israel's goal.

The Lady and the Tower of Babel

The cover of the book *Europe Is Rising* pictures the tower of Babel, a symbol commonly used by the Common Market, and includes these words, *"Europe--many tongues, one voice."* In the background, a modern crane leans against the ancient tower. In addition, the twelve stars of the Common Market are inverted, converting them into the sign of Satan. Just coincidence?

Canadian television aired a two-hour special called "Europe Unbounded," in which a united Europe was predicted to rule the world while the United States and Canada would be left powerless. During the program, some of the symbols of the united Europe were shown, including the tower of Babel and the image of a woman. Why are these symbols so important? According to the Bible, the last world political system will be composed part of iron and part of clay. What do these two parts represent?

Revelation 17 says that in the last days there will be a prostitute, a harlot, and she will commit fornication. She (religion) will sell herself to the kings of the world. In other words, religion and politics will join together. Why? To bring all men under one single government and one single religion.

What will be the foundation of this world religion? The New Age movement--the fastest growing religion in America today. In fact, it has already infiltrated churches, businesses, the media, sports, and even our schools. Children can learn how to visualize and have out-of-body experiences; they can be hypnotized; but they cannot pray to the God of all creation.

The present unity movement, under the guise of the New Age movement, is none other than the plan of the Antichrist and Satan. To understand how the world could be fooled into believing the lies of this satanic religion, we need to go back to the tower of Babel, where the New Age had its beginnings.

In Genesis 11 we read of an unnamed people building a great city on the plain of Shinar. To the narrator of this parable, peering across time and desert from his nomadic traditions, these folks were awesomely clever. Since they all spoke one common language, nothing was impossible for them. The plan of these ingenious people was to erect a huge tower whose top would reach to heaven. It would be an altar to their own intellect called Babel, or Gate of God. Their idea was to build a tower to God, to reach up and touch Him, so they, too, would become gods. The religion of Nimrod and Babel taught that we are all gods. An advertisement that appeared in the *Wall Street Journal* concerned the ancient tower of Babel and was presented as a parable. The ad stated:

> *"Babel or Gate of God, the God himself came down. Walked the streets of their cities, saw their project under construction. The arrogant race angered him. He passed his hand over the city, cursed it, now where there had been one language, suddenly there were hundreds. Con-*

fusion reigned. Nothing was possible.''

The ad said the lesson taught by this ancient parable is uncannily applicable for us in the twentieth century. They are saying, ''Listen, people, we have got to get together.'' Get it? If we can come together--if we can have one common language, government, and religion--nothing will be impossible for us.

Revelation 17 said in the last days there will be a harlot, a prostitute, who will sit on a beast; and she will ride across all the world. She will represent a religion that will bring everyone together. The harlot (the end-time religious system) will sit on the Beast (the Antichrist and his end-time dictatorship), and she will ride around the world collecting all peoples into one.

The Bible says that the harlot, the woman, will ride a beast. I used to think this parading harlot was just an accident until I ran across the front cover of the June 1975 edition of *Europe* magazine. Even then, it showed a Roman goddess riding on a beast as one of the official symbols of the Common Market. Accident? Not at all. One of the first stamps put out by the Common Market--a collective stamp used for the entire Common Market--showed the god of Europe riding on the back of a bull, begging to be worshipped. This is an exact picture of Revelation 17. The Bible says that when Europe finally gets to the position where it has all the power--economically, politically, and religiously--it will have but a short time to live. The New World Order will rule only one hour ,and will then give its power, strength, and might to the Beast.

The Antichrist

Telemarketing magazine ran an article addressing the future of Europe. Is Europe actually going to unite and work together in a unified form? The article states,

''I think it remains to be seen, but if it is going

*to work, a united Europe will need a leader.
Yes, only one overall leader to function effec-
tively. If they are going to work, they will have
to have one man who will head up the entire
thing."*

George Will, of the *Shreveport Journal,* writes an
article entitled, "Europe Moving Toward a Bureaucratic
State." You know what? He is right. Mr. Will says,

*"When I was in Washington, D.C. in early
1991, I saw a long line of limousines snaking
down the street in front of one of the city's
plush hotels. I asked a chauffeur who the
dignitary was. 'Ah,' he said, 'it is the president
of Europe.' The president of Europe? I didn't
know they had one. I discovered that he is not
really as much of a potentate as his title implies
or as he plans to be. But there is a president of
Europe who is appointed, not elected, to bring
about a political unity in Europe and around
the world. He has fifteen thousand employees
to help him."*

In Europe last year, I picked up a copy of a European
newspaper. The front page read, "The New Mr. Europe." It
stated that he will take over the presidency in January 1993, at
what (in theory) will be the dawn of a new Europe. It will be
a time when Europe will dominate and control the world.

Before all these events fully take place, the trumpet is
going to sound, and all true believers are going to be taken out
of this world. How do I know? Because the Bible says that is
exactly what is going to happen.

I really believe we are living near the end of time. If we
are the people who are going to see the last political system,

then the system cannot take over and rule until the Church is gone. We may see this last empire beginning to form, but it will not fully be in place until after the Rapture of the Church. That's why we as Christians must be different from any other people who have ever lived before. Jesus could come today to take every born-again person home to heaven.

When the Antichrist makes his appearance, he will speak great, swelling words of promise. I believe there will be people, maybe even someone reading this book, who will attend that first unholy Sunday. You and others may say after the great disappearing of the true Church, "Something is going on, and I have to find out what it is." The great orator, the Antichrist, will have magnificent, thrilling explanations for the disappearance of the millions of true Christians.

This tremendous, worldwide religious movement will bring all people into a single religion, and into one government with one economy exactly as prophesied in God's Word. The Apostle John saw two beasts. The first beast came out of the sea, that is, out of the Gentile world powers.

> "*I . . . saw a beast rise up out of the sea, having seven heads and ten horns, and upon his horns ten crowns, and upon his heads the name of blasphemy*" (Rev. 13:1).

The one who appears is the Antichrist. He will come up out of the kingdoms of the Gentiles.

The False Prophet

Just as there is a true Trinity, there is a false trinity. There is God, the Father; God, the Son; and God, the Holy Spirit. Satan's trinity puts him in the place of God; the Antichrist in the place of Jesus Christ; and an anti-prophet (or anti-spirit) in the place of the Holy Spirit.

In Revelation 13, we are introduced to this false

prophet. It appears to me that he comes up out of the land of Israel because in verse 11 we find,

> *"And I beheld another beast coming up out of the earth; and he had two horns like a lamb, and he spake as a dragon."*

Revelation says the land represents Palestine. What will be the purpose of the false prophet? Verse 12 explains,

> *"And he exerciseth all the power of the first beast before him, and causeth the earth and them which dwell therein to worship the first beast, whose deadly wound was healed."*

The first beast mocks death and resurrection. Notice, I said "mocks" because Satan does not have the power of resurrection. He is going to fake death and fake resurrection because he realizes that in order to be the Messiah, he must have a death with a resurrection. Therefore, he must fake it. The false prophet will give testimony to him saying, "Hey, look! He has died, and now he is resurrected!" Verse 14 states:

> *"And deceiveth them that dwell on the earth by the means of those miracles which he had power to do in the sight of the beast; saying to them that dwell on the earth, that they should make an image to the beast, which had the wound by a sword, and did live."*

Men will be delivered by miracles. The false prophet will be a great orator. He will do miracles. He will speak great, lying wonders. He will fake death and resurrection.

> *"And he had power to give life unto the image*

*of the beast, that the image of the beast should
both speak, and cause that as many as would
not worship the image of the beast should be
killed''* (vs. 15).

*''And there came one of the seven angels which
had the seven vials, and talked with me, saying
unto me, Come hither; I will shew unto thee the
judgment of the great whore that sitteth upon
many waters: With whom the kings of the earth
have committed fornication, and the inhabitants of the earth have been made drunk with the
wine of her fornication''* (Rev. 17:1-2).

You may ask, ''What are those waters?'' Let us now
consider Revelation 17:15:

*''And he saith unto me, The waters which thou
sawest, where the whore sitteth, are peoples,
and multitudes, and nations, and tongues.''*

In other words, it is a worldwide, false religious system. Verse
3 states,

*''So he carried me away in the spirit into the
wilderness: and I saw a woman sit upon a
scarlet coloured beast, full of names of blas-
phemy, having seven heads and ten horns.''*

Notice the similarity between the seven heads and ten horns--
the symbols of religion and government.

The Mark
At that point and time, according to Daniel 7, the
Antichrist will speak great and powerful things. He will do

miracles. People will begin to say, "Well, I guess this has got to be the Messiah." He will change the laws. He will change the times and the seasons. Everything will be different.

In Daniel we read how life will be under Antichrist:

> *"And the ten horns out of this kingdom are ten kings that shall arise: and another shall rise after them; and he shall be diverse from the first, and he shall subdue three kings. And he shall speak great words against the most High, and shall wear out the saints of the most High, and think to change times and laws: and they shall be given into his hand until a time and times and the dividing of time. But the judgment shall sit, and they shall take away his dominion, to consume and to destroy it unto the end"* (Dan. 7:24-26).

Revelation 13:16-18 also explains:

> *"And he causeth all, both small and great, rich and poor, free and bond, to receive a mark in their right hand, or in their foreheads: And that no man might buy or sell, save he that had the mark, or the name of the beast, or the number of his name. Here is wisdom. Let him that hath understanding count the number of the beast: for it is the number of a man; and his number is Six hundred threescore and six [or 666]."*

He will say, "Listen, if you are going to go to school, if you are going to buy food, if you are going to have a job, then you have to accept my mark."

I read an article written by a man who owns a company

that designs small electronic devices--minuscule silicone chips. When a dog or cat is taken to the veterinarian for a vaccination, a chip is placed in the animal's back with a wand, thus allowing authorities to be able to prove exactly who the pet's owner is. This is done to cattle in Canada, also. Incredibly, leading companies are now considering how soon these same chips can be implanted into people who perform various job functions. Cosmetically, the chip is concealed beneath the skin and is not noticeable. However, it does not escape the scanners that register all movement of those who go in and out of those areas being monitored. What a great way to ''brand'' people.

You know what? If you don't take the mark of the Antichrist (whether it is a chip or not, I don't know), you will not be able to buy or sell. You will not be able to hold a job or buy food at the grocery store. The Antichrist will require that everyone commit to him. I believe there is a coming mark, but only after the Rapture of the Church.

Right On Schedule

When Christ returns, He will defeat Antichrist and his cohorts. In Revelation 17:14 we read:

> ''*These shall make war with the Lamb, and the Lamb shall overcome them: for he is Lord of lords, and King of kings: and they that are with him are called, and chosen, and faithful.*''

Is the lamb a pretty good fighter? Not usually. This Lamb, however, is going to fight the Beast, and the Lamb is going to win. I believe the Lamb is none other than the Lamb of God, the person of Calvary, Jesus Christ. You see, history has recorded it. Reading on in Daniel 7:13-14, we find these words:

> ''*I saw in the night visions, and, behold, one*

like the Son of man came with the clouds of heaven, and came to the Ancient of days, and they brought him near before him. And there was given him dominion, and glory, and a kingdom, that all people, nations, and languages, should serve him: his dominion is an everlasting dominion, which shall not pass away, and his kingdom that which shall not be destroyed.''

Yes, friend, everything is right on schedule. Didn't the Bible say that Israel would be back in the land? Iraq would be destroyed once, twice, then devastated the last time? Is Germany reunited? Is Israel not reborn? Is Europe reconfiguring into a New Order, the Roman Empire reviving?

My dear friend, I believe we are living in the last days. No other generation who ever lived on planet earth has seen as much as you and I have seen. Subsequently, no other people who have ever lived are as accountable as we are. You and I are responsible for deciding whether we will spend eternity in heaven with Jesus Christ who died and rose again to save us, or whether we will spend an eternity in hell with Satan and his demonic fallen angels, for whom hell was created in order that sin can ultimately be purged and God's creation reconciled to Himself.

Jesus is the Prince of Life. Satan is the cannibal of death. You decide. Jesus is the truth and the life. Satan is the father of lies and the master of death. You decide.

Where Will You Spend Eternity?

The story is told of a man who once had a stray dog show up on his porch. He tolerated the dog for a day or two, then he decided he had to get rid of the critter. But the dog was faithful, and it followed him everywhere, no matter where he went or what he did. Frustrated by this faithful, old dog, the man said, "I have got to get rid of this dog."

He didn't have the heart to shoot the dog, so he loaded him into a simple row boat along with a big brick and rope. When he reached the middle of the lake, he called the faithful dog over to him, tied the rope around its neck, and the other end around the brick. Then he threw dog, brick, and rope into the lake. But the brick was not heavy enough to pull the dog all the way under!

Still being faithful, the old dog swam around and around and around the boat trying to get back to his master, all the while hauling the brick around with him. Now frustrated, the man felt he had to drown the dog somehow. He took an oar and began to hit the dog on the head, trying to poke it under the water. In the course of doing this, the man fell overboard into the lake, but he could not swim.

Seeing the man thrashing in the water himself, the dog came over, grabbed him by the collar, and began to swim toward the shore towing the brick, rope, and man. Finally, when the dog could swim no longer, the man put his feet down, only to find that he could now walk up on the bank. He looked back to find the brick had finally taken its toll on the dog--he had drowned.

When I heard this story, it made me think about a tale even more pathetic. I think an old man who would drown a dog is a pretty cruel man. But, I will tell you what is more cruel--for a person not to receive Christ! Jesus came to earth and did nothing but good. But some people don't want Him; they do everything they can to get rid of Him and keep Him out of their lives. They don't realize that the gospel is a story of love and faithfulness: *"For God so loved the world, that he gave his only begotten Son . . . "* (John 3:16). He sent His Son to die for you.

I don't know your heart's condition, but I do know that Jesus paid an incredible price to save you. He gave His life, and He did it willingly. If you have never received Christ as your personal Savior, then you need to make that decision today. Jesus allows you the option to say, "No, I don't want to be saved." He died for you; He arose again. The gospel is available, but He lets you say no--the choice is yours. Do you know what keeps a person from coming to Christ once they know they need Him? It is something called pride. Jesus Himself said, *"No man comes to the Father* [God] *but by me."* To be saved, simply admit to God that you are a sinner.

Dear friend, Christ came to this wretched, strife-torn, sinful world to save sinners. To qualify for the gospel of Jesus Christ, you have to be a sinner. And, you are a sinner whether you admit it or not. But, if you'll admit it, if you come to Christ who loves you so much He died for you, He will save you in an instant.

Instead of going through eternity in hell, where you and I deserve to go, you will live eternally in heaven, where God has a place reserved for you. Because of the sacrifice the Lord Jesus Christ made for you and me on that cruel Roman cross nearly two thousand years ago, you can live forever. Accept Him today. He is the only way.

Chapter Six

Messianic Expectations Among the Jews:
A Sign of the Last Days

J. Randall Price

Th.M., Ph.D.

When we say that we believe that these are the last days we do so only with the admonition of history ancient and modern. The ancient Jewish sages were greatly concerned over the misapplication of prophecy, not only because of erroneous interpretation provoking an unfounded confidence in a messianic claimant or inciting a revolutionary movement,[1] but for also a more basic spiritual reason. The Jewish scholar Rambam explains that the sages were troubled lest a predicted time comes and goes without the expected fulfillment. If that were to happen, people of insufficient faith would be induced to believe that the fulfillment would never come. The Jews had their share of failed predictions, from the proclamation of Bar Kokhba as Messiah in A.D. 132, to Shabbetai Zvi in the seventeenth century (he converted to Islam!). As a result, strict prohibitions against attempts to calculate or predict the end were included in the Talmud and Jewish writings. For example, we read of the warning to potential prognosticators:

> *"If you see that a man has prophesied the advent of the Messiah, know that he is engaged*

*either in sorcery or in dealings with devils.
. . . One has to say to such a man: 'Do not talk
in this manner.' . . . Eventually he will be the
laughingstock of the whole world.'*[2]

Christians have also made themselves the subject of the world's jokes by their failed calculations of the Rapture every *Rosh Ha-Shanah* (Jewish New Year, September/October). The most famous recent debacle was that led by the Koreans in 1992, whose campaign swept the globe and left thousands homeless (they had sold everything in preparation for the Rapture) and/or disillusioned. Today, books are on the shelves announcing the end will come in 1994[3] or the year 2000, and serious Christian interpreters must exercise caution in light of this trend toward sensationalism and speculation.

This admonition being heeded, we must nevertheless understand our times in light of the prophetic revelation. To err to some degree in our careful examination and application of God's Word is far better than to neglect it for fear of being wrong. After all, our Lord expected us to "discern the signs of the times" (Matt. 16:3), to "wait for" (1 Thess. 1:10), and "keep looking for" (Titus 2:13) the coming of Christ, activities that demand a constant scrutiny of both Scripture and the seasons. In this chapter I want to add my reasons to those of my prophetic colleagues as to why I believe these are indeed the last days. I have selected two recent events of prophetic significance that have occurred in the land of Israel, the focal point of all the prophetic plan. These are the signs of the revival of messianic revival and of the rebuilding of the Temple.

The First Sign: The Revival of Messianic Expectation

Not since the seventeenth century debacle surrounding the messianic claimant Shabbetai Zvi, has a revival of Jewish messianic expectation appeared on the scale of that recently displayed in the United States, England, Europe, and Israel.

Time[4] and *Newsweek* have both reported on the widespread publicity campaign of the Lubavitcher's campaign to prepare for the coming of the Messiah, a campaign which included books on the Jewish doctrine of the Messiah,[5] "prophetic" newsletters,[6] international newspaper advertisements,[7] banners, posters, electrified signs atop cars, and national messianic information hotlines[8] are among the many visible signs of this astounding movement.

The basis for this new messianism is in part drawn from Maimonides code of the Jewish law called the Principles of Faith. Number twelve of these thirteen fundamental principles reads:

> *"I believe with complete faith in the coming of Messiah. Though he tarry, nonetheless I await Him every day, that He will come."*

Such belief has been bolstered by the conviction that ours is the first age that has been identified for the realization of the messianic prophecies, and that recent events have demonstrated that they have been actualized and that the messianic redemption is at hand. A central feature of this modern messianic hope is the rebuilding of the Third Temple, for it is believed that through this climactic event the identity of the long-awaited Messiah will be finally revealed.

This messianic awakening, with its concomitant awareness that these are the final hours of Gentile domination (i.e., the "times of the Gentiles," Luke 21:24; cf. Rom. 11:25) before the Messiah arrives, is a signficant sign that we are living in the last days. This was a sign which Jesus Himself predicted for the time beginning the fulfillment of Daniel's seventieth week:

> *"For many shall come in my name, saying, I am Christ; and shall deceive many. . . . And*

*many false prophets shall rise, and shall de-
ceive many''* (Matt. 24:5,11)

After the Antichrist has revealed himself, Jesus predicted that such messianic identification will magnify itself with
convincing proofs:

> *''Then if any man shall say unto you, Lo, here
> is Christ, or there; believe it not. For there
> shall arise false Christs, and false prophets,
> and shall shew great signs and wonders;
> insomuch that, if it were possible, they shall
> deceive the very elect''* (Matt. 24:23-24).

The Origin of the Messianic Revival In Israel

The current messianic movement first began in Israel as
a response to the 1973 Yom Kippur War. In this war Israel was
surprised by an Egyptian attack and would have seen the Soviet
Union join with Arab allies had the war not been turned by U.S.
intervention in favor of the Israelis. In the aftermath of this
conflict an Orthodox Jew within the settlement group *Gush
Emunim* (''Bloc of the Faithful'') explained:

> *''We* [Jewish messianists[9]] *were born out of the
> Yom Kippur War. . . . Our Bibles told us that
> before Messiah comes, Israel will experience
> great distress. So while other Jews were de-
> pressed over the outcome of the war, we were
> encouraged. We believed this was the begin-
> ning of the redemption of Israel. Our belief is
> quite simple, really; when we possess all of the
> land historically held by the Jewish people, the
> Messiah will come. ''*[10]

As an example of the prophetic fervor surrounding the

Yom Kippur aftermath, a Rabbi Stein published a one hundred and twenty-five page book in Hebrew entitled *Magog: The War of Russia with Israel.* [11] This book was evidence of a widely held belief among many Jewish rabbis at that time, and many more since, that the end-time battle between Israel and an allied Russian-Arab league (Ezek. 38-39) was predicted to occur in our days. Rabbi Stein even suggested the date of 1994 in his book. About the mid-eighties, bumper stickers began appearing on the streets of Jerusalem that read "We Want Moshiah Now!" These were the product of the ultra-Orthodox hasidic group Habad, [12] whose two hundred and fifty thousand followers worldwide have propelled the messianic revival to international status.

The Messianic Movement's International Outreach

If the Yom Kippur War sparked the revival, all that was needed to set it on fire was the catalyst of another melé of prophetic proportions in the Middle East. The Gulf War was heralded as just such an event by those in the messianic movement, and was the momentum necessary to move the revival to international recognition. The religious authority which inspired this recognition was the Lubavitcher Rebbe, Rabbi Menachem Mendel Schneerson. The Talmud discusses the signs that will indicate the time that Messiah and the Day of Redemption is at hand in Sanhedrin 97-98, [13] and Schneerson declared that the present world conditions fit this description precisely. When the Gulf War hostilities were threatening Israel, Schneerson predicted that *"Israel would be the safest place in the world."* Although seventy-four Israelis died as a result of the Scud attacks, all but six died from heart problems, and it did indeed appear that Israel had been spared by God as Schneerson predicted.

International recognition of Schneerson's predictions was achieved by an aggressive campaign that targeted major newspapers and news magazines (as well as university campus' newspapers where a Habad student organization existed), with full-page ads. An example of one such ad that appeared in the *Jerusalem Post* pictured the word *Moshiach* ("Messiah" in Ashkenazi-accented Hebrew) as a connect-the-dot pattern, with each dot being a recent current event. The caption asked the reader to "Draw Your Own Conclusion." In the text of the ad the following statement was made:

> *"Yes, we are living in the most extraordinary times--as our world evolves toward a state of peace, and mankind thrives toward a state of perfection. The times are changing--not just for the better, but truly for the best. A cornerstone of Jewish faith is the belief that, ultimately, good and peace must triumph. This is the essence of 'Mosiach'--who will usher in the final redemption ordained in the Torah. The Lubavitcher Rebbe, Rabbi Menachem Mendel Schneerson, emphasizes that these remarkable events are merely the prelude to the final Redemption, culminating in unity among people, domestic harmony, and cessation of hostilities between races, neighbors, and nations. . . . The era of Mosiach is upon us.'"[14]*

Highly Visible Messianic Campaign In Israel

Leaders of the Lubavitchers in Israel announced that with the end of the war the Messiah would soon appear.[15] Throughout the Gulf War, banners on highways in Tel Aviv had read "Trust in HaShem (the Lord)," but these were soon replaced with the new banners, "Prepare for the Coming of Moshiah" emblazoned in black letters on one hundred foot yellow signs which depicted a red sun rising on the horizon. The purpose of these massive billboards, according to Menachem Brod, who spearheads public relations and publications for the

Habad Youth Organization in Israel, is *"to put Messiah into the national consciousness."* With thousands of Israeli motorists passing this sign daily the indoctrination is well underway. Brod, serious about the outcome of this "messianic campaign," stresses that getting people excited about the coming of Messiah and spurring them to action actually will hasten the arrival of the long-awaited era. In a *Jerusalem Post* interview, he announced to readers:

> *"Dear Jews, Moshiah is about to arrive! The dream of millions of Jews for centuries is upon us, and we all need to be ready for it!"* [16]

In this same vein, a paper distributed all over Israel entitled "Waiting In the Wings," the appeal is made to give Messiah the signal to come. The article in part reads:

> *"We must show him we want him with all our heart. He is ready. He is just waiting for the signal from us. Moshiach is waiting in the wings. He is ready. When he comes the curtain will rise on the most magnificent stage set we could imagine--world peace and disarmament, glory and honor for the Jews, the end of strife and jealousy. We must show him through our good deeds, through our tangible anticipation, through our longing for him, that we are ready."* [17]

In 1993 the banners, which still may be seen prominently displayed near the Western Wall, were supplemented with signs on street corners bearing pictures of Schneerson which read "Welcome King Messiah." To prepare for "Messiah Schneerson's" coming to Israel, a unique (for Israel) administration building, located in Kfar Habad, the movement's village near the Ben-Gurion airport on the Jerusalem-Tel Aviv highway, has been constructed. This building is an exact duplicate (inside and out) of the international headquarters building at 770 Eastern Parkway in Crown Heights, Brooklyn (New York), where Rabbi Schneerson presently resides.

While Schneerson has never been to Israel, he gave permission to his followers in March to begin building him a house in Kfar Habad. When he comes, his arrival will be heralded as the advent of the Messiah and the moment of redemption for Israel. Moshe Kruger, who participated in the ground breaking for the house, declared that this was a sign that the time is near: *"The Messiah will come any day!"* [18] Today, while Schneerson's campaign has moved to the background and the signs of messianic greeting have all but disappeared from street corners, this activity has marked a new chapter in Jewish history as a Jewish group has sought to identify the Messiah and indoctrinate their fellow Jews and Israelis concerning his coming.

The Coming Messianic Counterfeit and Israel

The interpretation of the Messiah as a strictly human, non-miracle-working, Jewish leader, has opened the field for many such messianic candidates. It has always been the expectation in Judaism that the Messiah would rebuild the Temple. This, in part, is based on the statement in Zechariah 6:12-13 which reads:

> *"And speak unto him, saying, Thus speaketh the Lord of hosts, saying, Behold the man whose name is The BRANCH; and he shall grow up out of his place, and he shall build the temple of the Lord: Even he shall build the temple of the Lord; and he shall bear the glory, and shall sit and rule upon his throne; and he shall be a priest upon his throne: and the*

counsel of peace shall be between them both. ''

Since this prediction was not fulfilled by Zerubbabel the priest and builder of the Second Temple, it became a text awaiting fulfillment by the future coming Messiah. Orthodox and ultra-Orthodox Jews expect this fulfillment in the rebuilding of the Third Temple when the Messiah makes his appearance in Jerusalem. Christians (with a dispensational perspective) expect this when Jesus as Messiah erects the Millennial (Fourth) Temple at the beginning of the Kingdom age.

In Israel, the owner of the Jerusalem Diamond Center, an ''Habadnik'' (follower of Habad), commissioned a photographic montage that depicted the rebuilt Third Temple standing on the modern Temple Mount with the new city in position all around. This photo was used in full-color, full-page advertisements by the Diamond Center in various magazines, such as El-Al airlines international in-flight magazine, and in full-color posters given away to customers at the Jerusalem Diamond Center. A framed copy of the photo adorns the entrance hallway of the Temple Institute in Jerusalem, the organization currently preparing the vessels for the new Temple.

Messianic movements such as that of the Lubavitchers is presently preparing the Jewish world to accept as Messiah whoever is instrumental in bringing about the erection of the Third Temple. Israeli Lubavitcher campaign leader Menachem Brod defines the Messiah as *''a great leader of the Jewish people; he will be such a great charismatic leader that the whole world will unite behind him. ''* However, Brod believes he will not be identified as Messiah immediately: *''the people may only realize that he has come after the fact--after we see his actions. ''* What actions are expected to be performed in confirmation of messiahship? Rabbi Manis Friedman, interviewed by University of Maryland professor Susan Handelman in the *Hasidic Journal Wellsprings*,[19] reveals the Lubavitch opinion:

"If he goes on to build the Temple and gather all Jews back to Israel, then we will know for sure that he is the Moshiach. Moshiach comes through his accomplishments and not through his pedigree. Maimonides says that once he builds the Temple and gathers the Jews back to Israel, then we will know for sure that he is the Moshiach. He doesn't have to say anything. He will accept the role, but we will give it to him. He won't take it to himself. And his coming, the moment of his coming, in the literal sense, would mean the moment when the whole world recognizes him as Moshiach . . . that both Jew and non-Jew recognize that he is responsible for all the wonderful improvements in the world: an end to war, an end to hunger, an end to suffering, a change in attitude." [20]

The Counterfeit Messiah and the Antichrist

The concept of the Messiah being accepted today is of a mortal man, a descendant of the Davidic dynasty, and a leader with sufficient charisma to capture and command the admiration of the world, if not its devotion. The timing for the arrival of this Messiah has been thought to be during a time of military threat to the Jewish people. Hasidic writer Naftali Lowenthal has observed that war has been an expected precursor to the advent of the Messiah. She writes:

"Throughout history Jewish leaders have seen international events and especially wars as expressing messianic portents. The book of Daniel prophesies wars as preceding the Messiah. The Midrash states, 'If you see nations battling together, you can expect the feet of the

Messiah' (Gen. Rab. 42:7). . . . Many Jews in our time saw the Second World War was the war of the 'birthpangs of the Messiah.' Recently the Gulf War excited similar speculation. . . . '[21]

While some aspects of the Hasidic Messiah have biblical basis, the expectation of a human leader who will arrive in a time of war, resolve the conflict in deliverance of Israel, and then rebuild the Temple, also fits the description given in the Old and New Testaments of the coming false messiah, the Antichrist. Since the Antichrist will probably be responsible for constructing the Third Temple through his covenant with Israel (Dan. 9:27), and since the expectation is that the Messiah will fulfill this role (Zech. 6:12), the Hasidic Jews may be preparing the Jewish people to accept the coming world (European) ruler (or likely his Jewish lieutenant, called the ''False Prophet'') as Messiah.

New Age Concepts In Hasidic Messianism

Aspects of the terminology used by the present Lubavitcher leadership to describe the spiritual responsibility people must take to bring the Messiah appears controlled by New Age concepts of reality. Rabbi Schneerson in a message based on Isaiah 11:9b: ''. . . *for the earth shall be full of the knowledge of the Lord, as the waters cover the sea,*'' said:

> ''*The prophet tells us that the redemption will herald a new reality for mankind. A reality in which the Divine intention underlying all of creation, and the Divine purpose inherent in everything, will become revealed to the world, enlightening all humankind.*'*[22]

One must wonder what such terms such as ''a new

reality," "inherent in everything," and "enlightening all humankind," have to do with the prophet's portrayal of a Millennial age where harmony is restored to the created order (Isa. 11:6-9a), and the Gentile nations submit to Messiah (Isa. 11:10)? Rabbi Friedman explains this New Age style of interpretation when he says:

> "The coming of Moshiach can't be one of these glassy-eyed, overwhelming experiences like the Exodus from Egypt or the giving of the Torah at Sinai, because those things just don't last. Because again, it's G-d doing it, not us. . . . It's just another good event in our long history of miracles and revelations. In order for Moshiach to come without disrupting us, without blowing us away, we have to have some awareness or some readiness, or some ability to handle the idea that the world is becoming good, that evil and suffering are going to end. Like the bumper sticker that says 'Visualize world peace.' So if you can't make it happen, visualize it; at least be able to conceive of it. So if we get more and more people thinking, 'Yes, it is time for the world to become good,' maybe we could actually realize that which everyone has always insisted and believed: that the world will some day be good.'"[23]

Friedman also believes that the world is progressing at the present time to achieve this potential state of Utopia:

> "In Yemos ha-Moshiach ('the Days of Moshiach') nature does not change. You don't have any resurrection of the dead, and you don't have any disruption of nature. All you

have is total universal goodness and morality.
And that would mean that nation does not
oppress nation, and that there is no suppres-
sion of religion, and so on. And we're begin-
ning to see that today.' [24]

Rabbi Schneerson has urged a similar course of action:

''Now he says the world is much closer to being
ready for Moshiach, but he says it depends on
us. If we expect more, if we ask the Holy One
to make it happen, it will.' [25]

What Friedman appears to be saying is that the messianic advent is always possible, but is not realized because it has
not been prepared for adequately by men. In Jewish history
miracles are the work of God--the initiation--but not the work
of man--the response. Therefore, the Messiah does not want to
come in an overwhelming and miraculous manner, but, as a
response to a world that has attained a new level of spiritual
reality--through visualizing a world of goodness--and working
at present to bring about a peaceful order politically and
religiously.

The Millennium envisioned by the biblical prophets is
indeed to be a world of righteousness (Hab. 2:14; Zech. 14:9),
but it comes by divine spiritual power (miraculous), not human
work (Zech. 4:6; 13:1-4; 14:3,9). The only ''millennium'' that
will come by human means will be the pseudo-peace brought
by the Antichrist during the first half of the Tribulation period.
Friedman has also noted that the core message of Moshiach is
teshuva (''repentance''):

''As Rav in Talmud (Sanhedrin 97b) stated
that all Jews need is to do 'teshuva' and
Moshiach comes, for all the predestined dates

for the redemption have already passed. '[26]

But what is the nature of this "repentance"? In the biblical context it will be in relation to their historical rejection of God's provision of redemption and their failure to place their faith in Him alone as Savior (Zech. 12:10-14), but that is far from Friedman's concept. He has in mind a return of worldwide Jewry, or at least a majority of the Jewish people, to biblical and Mishnaic legalism, and this will be made possible by the Antichrist's covenant with Israel.

There has never before existed such an extensive movement to prepare the Jewish people for wholesale allegiance to the Antichrist. Already it has contributed toward the Jewish recognition of the Messiah as a human political and religious figure whose calling card will be the rebuilding of the Temple. Indeed, in their own way, this revival may be hastening the day when that signal event will be realized.

The Second Sign:
The Revival of Efforts to Rebuild the Temple

Just as the revival of the messianic hope in Israel and among world Jewry a sign of the last days, so is its companion expectation, the rebuilding of the Temple. Since 1967, when Israel first acquired sovereignty over the Temple Mount, there has been unrelenting pressure on the Israeli government to create a Jewish presence there. In response to the unification of their ancient capital, and reclamation of the site of the Temple, Jewish groups in Israel and throughout the world began organizing efforts to raise funds and promote a movement to rebuild.[27] At the time, Jewish historian Israel Eldad prescribed a positive, yet more cautious posture:

> *"We are at the stage where David was when he liberated Jerusalem. From that time until the construction of the Temple by Solomon, only*

one generation passed. So will it be with us.''

The time from David's conquest of Jebusite Jerusalem until Solomon's building the Temple was approximately twenty-five years. Thus, the period of 1992-93 should correspond to this expected time, and what has occurred during these years has been interpreted by many prophetic scholars as setting in motion events that will inevitably lead to the rebuilding of the Temple.[28]

Present Political Conditions and the Rebuilding of the Temple

In 1992 Israeli Temple activism dramatically increased, motivated in part by fear that increased political pressure on the Israeli government from the world community would force territorial concessions in East Jerusalem, forever removing the possibility of reclaiming religious access to the Temple Mount. When in 1993 we saw Israel's Labor Party sign the ''Declaration of Principles'' with that faction of the PLO under Yasser Arafat, these fears became reality. The direction of these two opposite purposes will ultimately result in conflict, as can be seen from recent events.[29]

On the Arab side, since the accord, both Arafat and Jordan's King Hussein have publicly stated that Jerusalem is the goal of their negotiations. For example, King Hussein (who still considers East Jerusalem Jordanian territory) recently declared: *''Jerusalem is the essence of peace between us.''*[30] Being interpreted, this means that there can never be any peace in the Middle East until Israel relinquishes all claims to Jerusalem. Indeed, the return of Jerusalem is a sacred call by Iran's Islamic revolutionary government as well as by militant Islamic fundamentalist organizations throughout the world. Arafat has said that he will not rest until the Palestinian flag flies over Jerusalem (the proclaimed capital of the Palestinian state) and the hill of *as-Shakra* (the Dome of the Rock) and *al-Aqsa* (the

Muslim mosque) are sovereign Arab territory once again.

On the Israeli side, a council of seventy Jewish leaders has recently affixed their signature to a document entitled ''The Covenant of Jerusalem.'' This agreement signed on Jerusalem Day, May 9, 1993, and affirmed by Jews worldwide, is modelled after the covenant made by the returning Judean exiles to restore Jerusalem and rebuild the Temple. It states unequivocally that the city *''links heavenly Jerusalem with earthly Jerusalem''* and that the Temple Mount is the site of the future Temple, citing Isaiah 2:2-4.[31] Since Jerusalem was restored in 1967, this agreement is, in effect, a pledge to see the Third Temple rebuilt. Because of this, some prophetic thinkers have suggested that this document may be the basis for the ultimate agreement between Israel and the Antichrist (cf. Dan. 9:27).[32] Whether or not this proves to be the case, such a ''covenant'' has certainly set the course for all future peace negotiations concerning the city of Jerusalem. At the same time, despite the euphoria of the rest of the world concerning the prospect of peace in the Middle East, weapons (including nuclear weapons technology) continue pouring into the United Arab Emirates, and especially into Iran, Syria, and Saudi Arabia from such places as Russia and Europe.[33]

The prospect of such an encounter over the Temple Mount was shown to the world shortly before the Gulf War. The ''Temple Mount Incident'' of October 8, 1991 made international headlines and brought the condemnation of the United Nations for ''Israel aggression'' in the deaths of seventeen Palestinian Arabs. These terrorists had been killed on the area of the Temple Mount platform overlooking the Western Wall Plaza, for stoning Jewish worshippers at the Wall below. What had incited the riot was an announcement by the Temple Mount Faithful, one of the most activist organizations in the Temple movement, that they would attempt to lay a cornerstone for the Third Temple. As a result, it is said that that morning the loudspeakers that normally sound the Muslim call to prayer, exhorted tens of thousands of Moslems to *"come to the Mount and sacrifice soul and blood to save the land"* and to *"prevent the occupation of Islam's holy places."*[34] As world opinion turned against Israel for the riot, Saddam Hussein, who had only two months earlier invaded Kuwait, used the situation to Iraqi advantage, announcing that he would not withdraw from Kuwait until Israel withdrew from the "occupied Arab lands." Saddam's ultimate objective was to return Saudi Arabia and Egypt to the cause of *jihad* (holy war) against Israel, with himself as the successor to Iraq's only leader to ever conquer Israel, the Babylonian king Nebuchadnezzar.

To this end, Saddam launched his Scud missiles against Tel Aviv in hopes that Israel would retaliate and force the Arab League to unite against her. Apart from the restraint Israel exercised in this encounter, the entire Middle East would have become engulfed in a major conflict, ultimately committing the world powers to an engagement on the scale of an Armageddon. While war was averted on this occasion, it is important to note that any such demonstration of desire by Israelis for a return to the Temple Mount constitutes a war against Islam and their claim to the land. The Arabs view the Temple Mount issue as the paramount issue, politically and religiously, and recognize that a rebuilding of the Jewish Temple would be the conclusive act assuring Israeli sovereignty over Israel. For this reason the Temple Mount is now at the center stage for any negotiations between Israel and the Arab League, and will become the focus of greater conflicts in the days ahead.

The Current Activities in Preparation for Rebuilding

In my book co-authored with Thomas Ice, *Ready to Rebuild: The Imminent Plan to Rebuild the Last Days Temple* (Harvest House, 1992), I have surveyed the various individuals and organizations which formed what is now called "the Temple movement." We refer the reader there to details of organizations such as the priestly school of *Ateret Cohanim*, the researchers and artisans of the Temple Institute who have created some fifty vessels and implements for restored Temple worship, the activities of the Temple Mount and Eretz-Israel Faithful, who continue to demonstrate for access to the Temple Mount, and *Atara Leyoshna*, who have bought and established a Jewish presence at Judaism's most sacred spot on earth. What I will highlight here will be those events of the Temple movement that have occurred since the publication of that previous research.

Jewish Fundamental Society

Rabbi Nahman Kahane, the brother of the late Kach Party leader Meir Kahane, and head of the Young Israel Synagogue (the closest synagogue to the Temple Mount) and the Institute for Talmudic Commentaries, has long been at the forefront of religious efforts to see the Temple rebuilt. For years his activities were scholarly in nature, and he publicly distanced himself from activist organizations, choosing rather to quietly compile a computerized list of all qualified *cohanim* ("priests") in Israel. Recently, however, he has shifted to a semi-activist stance and reported the formation of a Jewish fundamentalist organization in response to those existing in Christian and Islamic circles.[35] He has stated seven goals for this organization which are:

1. The return of the Israeli nation to a monarchy;
2. The return of the Israeli people to a classic Jewish (biblical) lifestyle;
3. The restoration of the Sanhedrin to elect a high priest;
4. The formation of a government with a reigning prophet;
5. The liberation of all the land promised to

Israel;
6. The making G-d the center of the universe;
   and
7. The rebuilding of the Third Temple.

Kahane's move from a passive to a more activist position is indicative of the new acceleration within the Temple movement under the new Labor government that now threatens a reversal of the gains made under the former Likud government. Like Rabbi Joel Lerner of the Sanhedrin Institute, and Rabbi Shlomo Goren, former Ashkenazi chief rabbi who has constructed a fully-furnished meeting place for the restored Sanhedrin adjacent to the Temple Mount, Rabbi Kahane advocates returning to the rule of Sages with a Torah-based government, which must--in order to *properly* perform--exist in relation to a functioning Temple.

Reviving an Ancient Jewish Ceremony on the Temple Mount

Reuven Prager, the founder of *Beged Ivri* (''Hebrew Clothing'') believes that it is his destiny to assist in returning Israelis and all Jews to a biblical lifestyle in preparation for the advent of the ''Third Temple era.'' Indeed, a sign with just such an announcement greets visitors to Prager's shop in the ultra-Orthodox Jewish section of Jerusalem. A Temple Mount activist in his own right, he has worked for years toward the revival of an ancient Jewish marriage ceremony which takes place on the Temple Mount. Prager explains the reason for this revival:

> ''*Between the First and Second Temple period, there existed an ancient marriage ceremony which was performed primarily in Jerusalem. This beautiful and colorful event fell into disuse after the destruction of the*

*Second Temple and the loss of the Land. With
the return of the Jewish people to the Land of
Israel, preparations are paving the way for the
establishment of the Third Temple and with
them, the revival of Temple consciousness--
hence the . . . proposal for the reinstitution of
the ancient Jewish marriage ceremony.* '[36]

To realize this goal, Prager established a non-profit
organization registered with the Ministry of the Interior, had
constructed the ancient bridal crown made of pure gold, and
raised funds to build the *apiron* or royal wedding litter,
originally described in the Song of Solomon. With the comple-
tion of the *apiron* last year, Prager has successfully entertained
numerous Jewish families outside of Israel with the prospect of
conducting their weddings in Jerusalem on the Temple Mount.
His belief, like all in the Temple movement, is that increased
religious devotion (the fulfillment of *mitzvot*, "command-
ments") toward the Temple will hasten the day of its rebuilding.

The Establishment of the Temple Mount Yeshiva

With the beginning of the new Jewish year (*Rosh
Hashana* 5754/September 1993) a new institution, the first of
its kind in two thousand years, is functioning on the Temple
Mount with more than twenty active students. This new
institution is the Temple Mount *Yeshiva* (religious school),
organized in March of 1993 by Kach activist Baruch Ben Yosef
to daily study Talmud on the site of the Temple.[36] In a position
paper available from their headquarters next to the Temple
Institute, they state their purpose for organizing:

*"The Yeshiva of the Temple Mount has been
established as a prerequisite to the full liberation of Judaism's most holy cite (sic). We, the*

founders of Yeshivat Har HaBayit, understand that the government of Israel has little, if any, concern regarding the future of what must become the center of Jewish thought and activity. We are also aware of the current overwhelming and tragic anxiety felt by most Israelis over the willingness of the government to relinquish control of the liberated lands of 1967. Therefore, we have taken the burden upon ourselves to maintain and build upon the gifts given to our generation. That is to say, the Yeshiva of the Temple Mount intends to be the catalyst of change. We decided several months ago that the status quo on the Temple Mount cannot continue. The answer, we believed, was to put into operation the Yeshiva of the Temple Mount. We are training a generation of Jews that will know the laws of the Temple and prepare for its rebuilding. Our Yeshiva will not allow this pivotal issue to leave the agenda of the Jewish people. In spite of the harsh conditions imposed by the government and the Moslem Religious Council, we continue to work for the liberation of the Temple Mount for we know that the disaster of our Holy Mount is the source of our problems.'[37]

The directors of the *yeshiva* do not agree with the widely-held Orthodox Jewish belief (currently represented by Sephardi chief rabbi Mordechai Eliahu) that the Third Temple will descend (miraculously) from heaven in fire. They would agree with Rabbi Yisrael Ariel of the Temple Institute, who has stated that such belief comes from the Jewish apocryphal writings and the New Testament (cf. Rev. 21:2,10), rather than from traditionally-accepted Jewish texts.[38] Following the ancient Jewish legal expert Maimonides, the Temple Mount *Yeshiva* calls for the people of Israel to obey the biblical and rabbinic obligation to rebuild the Temple themselves. In fact, they believe that divine punishment of *Kareit* (''cutting off [of the soul]'') will result from the failure to rebuild the Temple and offer the Passover sacrifice. Therefore they conclude their position paper with an imperative:

> *''There is but one way to redeem the Temple Mount and but one way to renew the sacrifices and build the Temple. 'Action'! Just as we witnessed the destruction of six million Jews because of the inaction concerning the return to Zion, so will we endure terrible tragedy should we opt for the same inaction concerning the Temple Mount.... The fate and destiny of the Jewish people and their redemption are in the hands of each and every Jew. All that is required is will and faith of Jews to enter the Temple Mount until we have the numbers to demand its return to its rightful owners. If every one would make the commitment needed to redeem the Mount it will surely be speedily in our hands.'* [39]

The Temple Mount *Yeshiva*, like so many other of the organizations in the Temple movement, which is gaining new ground each year, represents a new generation of Israelis who are more religious and radically determined to see Israel return to its biblical heritage and purpose. Their zeal may well be one of the factors that not only invites the coming conflict with the Arabs, but afterward compels them to make a covenant with the Antichrist allowing for the rebuilding of the Temple.

The Renewed Search for Temple Treasures

In conjunction with the efforts to rebuild the Temple is the present search for lost Temple treasures.[40] An ancient Jewish tradition taught that before the rebuilding of the Temple, the treasures of the Temple, removed from it before its destruction in A.D. 70, will be discovered and restored. Some rabbis taught that this would be the task of the Messiah, and would be one of the signs of his authentication. Others have taught that Gentiles would be involved in recovering these objects, since there are cryptic allusions to Gentile gifts and assistance in rebuilding the Temple (cf. Isa. 18:7; 56:6-7; 60:10; Zech. 6:15; Hag. 2:7). Jewish tradition held that the Tabernacle, the incense altar, and the Ark of the Covenant with Aaron's rod, the pot of manna, and the Tablets of the Law, were all hidden within a secret compartment beneath the Chamber of Wood on the west side of the Temple, close to the Holy of Holies.

The Discovery of the Ark of the Covenant?

Recently, two Jewish rabbis, Rabbi Yehuda Getz and Rabbi Shlomo Goren, made the startling announcement that the entrance to this compartment has been discovered in excavations at the Warren's Gate in the Western Wall Tunnel beneath the present Western Wall Plaza. While the Warren's Gate itself has been shut and sealed by the Israeli government, these rabbis, as well as those at the Temple Institute, where a new model of the Ark is now prominently displayed, believe that the day is at hand in which these treasures will be revealed to the world.

The Search for the Ashes of the Red Heifer

Meanwhile, other efforts have been mounted to locate the ashes of the red heifer which from antiquity were sealed in a stone jar. Geophysical investigation of the Qumran plateau overlooking Cave IV (thought to be the site of the Wadi Ha-

Kippa) using ground-penetrating radar has recently revealed exciting anomalies that have been identified as an urn with ashes, metal, scrolls, and pottery.[41] While exploratory trenches dug on the site to examine these anomalies were stopped by military authorities, legal action on behalf of the research organization is seeking to re-open the dig. In a recent newsletter from the supporting organization the following was stated:

> *"If we should find the ashes of the red heifer (Num. 19) and also the Tabernacle of David (Acts 15:16; Amos 9:11), how long would it take to set up Temple worship? . . . We will . . . try to expedite all* [legal] *matters so that the dig can be completed before the PLO takes charge of the area.'"[42]*

Similar excavations continue to be pursued by Vendyl Jones, whose dig at the Cave of the Columns was closed by the Israeli Antiquities Authority after a large quantity of a substance claimed to be Temple incense was discovered in March of 1992.

Conclusion

Perhaps one of these excavations will unearth Temple treasures in the near future that will introduce a new threat to the Muslim authorities controlling the Temple Mount. Perhaps the rabbis will surprise the Arab world with the revelation of the Ark of the Covenant and force a conflict over final possession of the site of the Temple. If we join these activities with the revival of messianic expectation, we have two significant signs corresponding to what Scripture has predicted would occur at the time of the end. Whatever the present outcome, we may be sure that these events are hastening the day of the Lord's coming. May they serve to awaken each of us to the fact that we are living in the last days!

Notes

1. Cf. Flavius Josephus, *Wars of the Jews* (Book IV): "But what more than anything else incited them to war was an ambiguous oracle [probably Daniel 7:13-14 or 9:26], likewise found in their sacred scriptures, to the effect that at that time one from their country would become ruler of the world. This they misunderstood to mean someone of their own race, and many of their wise men went astray in their interpretation of it. The oracle, however, in reality signified the sovereignty of Vespasian, who was proclaimed Emperor on Jewish soil."

2. *Sefer Hasidim*, edited by J. Wistinetzki (1924), 76-77, no. 212.

3. Cf. Howard Kamping's *1994*.

4. Lisa Beyer, "Expecting the Messiah," *Time* (March 23, 1992), p. 49; Kenneth Woodward and Hannah Brown, "Doth My Redeemer Live?" *Newsweek* (April 27, 1992), p. 53.

5. Two of the most widely circulated are Rabbi Abraham Stone, *Highlights of Moshiach Based Upon the Talmud, Midrash, and Classical Rabbinical Sources*, and Rabbi Jacob Immanuel Schochet, *Mashiach: The Principle of Mashiach and the Messianic Era in Jewish Law and Tradition*.

6. While Hasidic magazines such as *Chai Today, Wellsprings*, and *L'Chaim*, etc. all carry articles relating to the present messianic expectation, a newsletter devoted entirely to the issue called *Moshiach Matters* has recently been published by the International Campaign to Help Bring Moshiach.

7. E.g. full-page ads in the *New York Times* announced, "The Time of Your Redemption Has Arrived."

8. An introduction to the Jewish concept of the Messiah is available by dialing 1-800-4-MOSHIACH in the United States and 1-800-2-MASHIACH in Canada. The message, a four-minute mini-class (in English) is changed weekly. A more detailed daily message can be heard by dialing (708) 953-6168 (in English, Hebrew, or Yiddish). With all hotlines, questions can be left for return information calls. For those interested in contacting the international campaign headquarters in New York, call (718) 778-6000.

9. Throughout this article the term *Jewish messianist* will be used rather than *messianic Jew*, although the latter is that most used in Israel. The substitution is made to avoid confusion with Jews who believe in Jesus as Messiah, commonly referred to by this term especially in the United States.

10. As cited in the article "Messianic Moods" by Elwood McQuaid, *Moody Monthly*.

11. Rabbi S. Stein, *Magog: The War of Russia with Israel* (Jerusalem, 1974).

12. The name "Habad" is actually an acronym for H = *chokmah* ("wisdom"), b = *binah* ("understanding"), d = *da'at* ("knowledge"). The "a" vowels are only supplied for readability; the Hebrew consonants alone make the word.

13. Ten signs are listed as: (1) the world is either righteous or guilty; (2) the truth is in short supply; (3) inflation skyrockets; (4) Israel will have begun to be repopulated according to Ezekiel 36:8-12; (5) wise people will be scarce; (6) the Jews will have despaired of redemption; (7) the young will be contemptuous of the old; (8) scholarship will stink; (9) piety will be in disgust; and (10) a growing number of Jews will turn on their people. For a discussion of these signs cf., Moshe Kohn, "The Do-Gooders Are Holding Up Messiah," *Jerusalem Post International Edition*, August 15, 1992, p. 13.

14. *Jerusalem Post International Edition*, August 31, 1991.

15. Cf. "Debate Splits Lubavitcher Hasidim: Is the Messiah Now Among Them?" *New York Times*, Friday, January 29, 1993, p. A14.

16. *Jerusalem Post Weekend Magazine*, October 5, 1991, p. 13

17. As cited in *End-Time Magazine*, July-August 1992, p. 17.

18. *Newsweek*, April 27, 1992, p. 53 (top third column)

19. *Wellsprings* (A Quarterly Journal for Exploring the Inner Dimensions of Torah and Jewish Life, published by the Lubavitch Youth Organization), Winter 1992, pp. 20-28. This entire issue is devoted exclusively to articles dealing with the Messiah.

20. *Ibid*, p. 20. The citation referred to by Maimonides reads: "The King Messiah will arise and return the Kingship of the House of David to its former power. He will build the Temple, and gather the Jews scattered in Exile. In his time all (Jewish) laws will come back into force."

21. *Ibid*, p. 17.

22. R. Menachem M. Schneerson, "A Changing Reality," *Lubavitch International*, Winter 1993, p. 3.

23. *Wellsprings*, December 1992, p. 27

24. *Ibid*, p. 24

25. *Jerusalem Post*, October 5, 1991, p. 13.

26. *Ibid*, p. 22.

27. Cf. ad that appeared before Six-Day War in the *Washington Post*, May 21, 1967, and statements of Rabbi Sinai Halberstam, "The Beth Hamildosh," in *The Jewish Press*, August 2, 1968, pp. 19-20.

28. Cf. e.g., "Prophecy Scholars Debate Signs of Armageddon in Mideast," Associated Press release, September 25, 1993.

29. For an extensive review of the political history of conflict between these perspectives cf. Roger Friedland and Richard D. Hecht, "The Politics of Sacred Places: Jerusalem's Temple Mount/al-haram al-sharif," in *Sacred Places and Profane Spaces: Essays in the Geographics of Judaism, Christianity, and Islam.* Edited by Jamie Scott and Paul Simpson-Housley (New York: Greenwood Press, 1991), pp. 21-61.

30. Cf. "Separating Religion, Politics Called Answer to Status of Jerusalem," *Washington Post* Service release, September 27, 1993.

31. Cf. the reproduction of this document in *Israel Scene* magazine, a supplement to the *Jerusalem Post*, May 29, 1993.

32. Cf. e.g., Gary Stearman, "The Covenant of Jerusalem Is Signed!" *End-Time Magazine*, September-October 1993, pp. 6-12; and Irvin Baxter, "Is This the 'Covenant of Daniel 9:27'?" p. 13.

33. Cf. "Weapons Still Pouring Into Middle East," Associated Press release, August 12, 1993.

34. Finding of the Zamir Commission reported by David Bar-Illan in an article entitled "Temple Mount Provocation," *Jerusalem Post International Edition*, August 10, 1991, p. 7.

35. Reported by Jimmy DeYoung after a phone conversation with Rabbi Kahane on October 16, 1992.

36. Cf. "Temple Mount Yeshiva," *In Jerusalem* (a publication of *Jerusalem Post*), vol. 17, no. 22, Friday, May 28, 1993, p. 1.

37. Cover page, "Position Paper" (published by The *Yeshiva* of the Temple Mount), 1993.

38. Cf. "Temple Will Be Man-Made," *Jerusalem Post International Edition*, August 28, 1993, p. 3.

39. "Position Paper," p. 7.

40. For complete details on this subject see my new book, *In Search of Temple Treasures: The Lost Ark and the Last Days* (Harvest House Publishers) to be released Fall 1994.

41. Cf. Zvi ben-Avraham and Uri Basson, "Geophysical Investigation of the Qumran Plateau Using Ground-Penetrating Radar and Seismic Reflection Profiles" (Tel Aviv University: Department of Geophysics and Planetary Sciences, 1992), pp. 3-5; Aubrey L. Richardson, Sr. and Garold R. Collett, "Qumran: Summary Excerpts of Research and Reports from 1988 through 1990" (updated edition, November-December 1990), p. 12 (attachment B).

42. Paul Snyder, *Jerusalem/Mitzvah International Newsletter*, November 1993.

Chapter 7

Gog and Magog 1993

Mark Hitchcock

Students of Bible Prophecy have generally agreed that Ezekiel 38-39 predicts that in the last days a great horde of nations, led by the Soviet Union, will swoop down into the land of Israel to cash in on Israel's wealth, control the Middle East, and challenge Antichrist's authority. However, at the end of 1991 and early part of 1992 the world witnessed an unforeseen, unbelievable event--the dissolution of the Soviet Empire. This single event has affected our world in every way imaginable: politically, militarily, religiously, and economically. The event has been heralded by many as the beginning of a new world order, a world without the ominous threat of communism hanging over its head.

For some students of Bible prophecy, however, this event has led to confusion and doubt. Many have been left wondering if God's Word is untrue or if trusted Bible scholars have totally misinterpreted Ezekiel 38-39. When one carefully examines the nations and events in Ezekiel 38-39, it is readily apparent that the fall of the Soviet Union has not proved the Bible untrue; rather, it has created an incredible scenario that makes the fulfillment of Ezekiel 38-39 more certain and imminent than ever before!

The fall of the Soviet Union has left a great power

vacuum in central Asia and the Middle East and this vacuum is being filled by militant, fundamentalist Islam. I believe that these events are happening in preparation for the great invasion of Israel in the end-times foretold by the Jewish prophet Ezekiel twenty-six hundred years ago.

The Soviet Empire has ended, but a new empire seems to be rising from its ashes. The new empire is not the new commonwealth or the former Russian republic--the new empire is the great Islamic wave.

Amazing events are occurring in our world today, especially the Moslem world, even as these words are being written. Never before in history have world events changed more suddenly or dramatically from the perspective of Bible prophecy. Never have so many biblically relevant factors converged more clearly.

The former southern republics of the Soviet Union are all Moslem nations except the Ukraine, Armenia, and Georgia. The Moslem nations are Azerbaijan, Kazakhstan, Uzbekistan, Kirghizia, Turkmenistan, and Tajikistan. These six new nations make up twenty-one percent of the population of the old Soviet Union, or a total population of fifty-seven million. The fall of the Soviet Union has spawned the existence of six new, powerful, independent Moslem nations.

These newly independent nations have three main things in common. First, as already noted, they are all Moslem. Second, they all lack hard currency. Third, they all have nuclear weapons within their boundaries and at their disposal. These three factors are obviously a dangerous combination. The scenario is clear: these six republics will conspire with their Islamic brothers in Iran, Syria, Pakistan, Libya, and Turkey to exchange nuclear devices for hard currency. The common bond that binds them together is their common commitment to destroy Israel.

This scenario is already beginning to develop as we see these new Moslem nations forming alliances with other nations, and many of these Moslem nations are also developing close ties with one another. At least one Moslem nation has purchased nuclear weapons from one of the newly independent Moslem republics. These alliances and activities could be the direct fulfillment of Ezekiel 38 and 39!

Experts on Middle East affairs are proclaiming a powerful new surge in militant Islam in the Middle East.

So what is the cause of this sudden rise in militant Islam? Experts agree that two explosive events in the last year have served as catalysts for the new rise of Islam. These two events are the Persian Gulf war and the collapse of the Soviet Union and communism.

Communism was the strongest opponent to militant Islam in the Middle East. Therefore, the fall of the Soviet Union and communism has thrown the door wide open for militant Islam to rise like a shooting star in the Middle East.

The breakup of the Soviet Union has caused a dramatic power shift that affects every area of the world. The world has not been stabilized by the fall of the Soviet Union; it has been greatly destabilized. Three major factors have contributed to the balance of power that has existed in the world for several decades:

1. there were only two major players (the U.S. and the Soviet Union);
2. both were in approximate balance; and
3. both were considered rational.

Now the balance of power has been thrown into confusion. There are no longer two players involved in the balance of power formula, there are over a dozen. The world is more at risk for a global holocaust than at any time in history. Nuclear weapons are being distributed and are falling into the hands of irrational, fanatical leaders! The foment in the Islamic world could ignite at any time into a *jihad*, or holy war.

Gog and Many Peoples With Him

Ezekiel 38 describes a great coalition of nations that will invade the land of Israel when Israel is regathered and resting in her land (Ezek. 38:8,11,14).

> *"After many days thou shalt be visited: in the latter years thou shalt come into the land that is brought back from the sword, and is gathered out of many people, against the mountains of Israel, which have been always waste: but it is brought forth out of the nations, and they shall dwell safely all of them. Thou shalt ascend and come like a storm, thou shalt be like a cloud to cover the land, thou, and all thy bands, and many people with thee. . . . And thou shalt come from thy place out of the north parts, thou, and many people with thee, all of them riding upon horses, a great company, and a mighty army: And thou shalt come up against my people of Israel, as a cloud to cover the land . . ."*(Ezek 38:8-9,15-16).

There are ten names listed in Ezekiel 38:1-6, which represent several modern nations that are presently forming alliances with one another. As we consider these nations, I think you will be amazed to see who they are and how they are developing close military and economic ties to one another.

Gog

The first name mentioned in the list of nations in Ezekiel 38:1-6 is Gog. The name Gog means "high, supreme, a height, or a high mountain." The way the name is used in Ezekiel 38-39 certainly reveals that Gog is a person, not a place. Ezekiel says that Gog is "of the land of Magog" and is "the chief prince of Meshech and Tubal" (Ezek 38:2). This language shows clearly that Gog is a person from the land of Magog who is the prince or ruler of Meshech and Tubal.

Magog

Ancient Magog has been identified with several groups of people. However, the most likely identification of Magog is provided by the Jewish historian Josephus who said, *"Magog founded the Magogians, thus named after him, but who by the Greeks are called Scythians."* This identification was adopted by the Church fathers Jerome and Theodoret. It has also been almost universally accepted by conservative students of Bible prophecy.

The descendants of ancient Magog--the Scythians--were the original inhabitants of the plateau of Central Asia, and later some of these people moved into the area north of the Black Sea. The homeland of the ancient Scythians is inhabited today by the former Soviet republics of Kazakhstan, Kirghizia, Uzbekistan, Turkmenistan and Tajikistan. All of these former Soviet republics are now independent nations, and they are all Moslem nations who are being courted by their Moslem neighbors in Iran and Turkey.

All of these new Central Asian nations speak Turkic languages, except Tajikistan, where the language is similar to Iranian Farsi. Iran is presently involved in the civil war that is raging in Tajikistan, training rebels and sending them into Tajikistan to spread Iran's fundamentalist Islamic gospel among the Moslems in Central Asia. Iran has also purchased nuclear weapons from Kazakhstan. This alliance is forming before our eyes!

Turkey is wooing the Moslem nations of Central Asia by offering ten thousand scholarships to young men in these nations and giving the region $1.1 billion in agricultural credits and investment guarantees. Turkey has economic, linguistic, religious, political, and emotional ties to the new Moslem nations of Central Asia and is developing ties with them in fulfillment of Ezekiel 38-39.

Rosh

Another nation that will be allied with Iran in her coming invasion of Israel is Rosh. The Hebrew word *rosh* simply means head, top, summit, upper part, chief, total, or sum. It is a very common word and is common to all Semitic languages. It occurs approximately seven hundred and fifty times in the Old Testament along with its roots and derivatives. The meaning of this word has led many Bible scholars to translate the word rosh here, not as a proper name, but simply as ''chief.'' They translate Ezekiel 38:2b, ''the chief prince of Meshech and Tubal.'' The King James Version, the Revised Standard Version, New American Bible and the New International Version all adopt this translation.

The great weight of evidence, however, favors taking Rosh as a proper name of a geographical location. The great Hebrew scholars C.F. Keil and Wilhelm Gesenius both state clearly that the word Rosh in Ezekiel 38:2-3; 39:1 is a proper name of a geographical location. The Septuagint, the Greek translation of the Old Testament, translates the Hebrew *rosh* as the proper name Ros. This point is especially important since the Septuagint was translated only three centuries after the Book of Ezekiel was written. Many Bible dictionaries and encyclopedias also support this view: *The New Bible Dictionary*, *The Wycliffe Bible Dictionary*, and *The International Standard Bible Encyclopedia*.

Another point in favor of identifying Rosh with a geographical location rather than as a title is its recurrence in Ezekiel 38:3 and 39:1. If Rosh were simply a title it probably would be dropped in these two places because when titles are repeated they are generally abbreviated.

The most impressive evidence in favor of taking Rosh as a proper name is simply that this translation is the most accurate. The phrase in Ezekiel 38:2 should therefore be translated "the chief of Rosh, Meshech and Tubal." This is the most natural way of rendering the Hebrew in this passage. Several well known translations of the Bible agree with this view. Rosh is translated as a proper name in the Jerusalem Bible, the New English Bible and the New American Standard Bible.

Having found that Rosh is a proper name, the next question we must ask is, to whom or what does the name Rosh refer? Is Rosh Russia or should we look somewhere else?

In all three of its occurrences the word Rosh is listed with Meshech and Tubal under the rule of Gog. The only indication the Bible gives us of the location of these names is that they come from the " north parts" (38:15, 39:2).

Two of Gog's other allies, Gomer and Togarmah, are also said to come from "the north quarters" (38:6). Rosh is linked in Ezekiel 38-39 both militarily and geographically with other nations from the remotest parts of the north. We know, therefore, that seven of the ten nations mentioned in Ezekiel 38:2-6, including Rosh, come from the far north.

While this information from the Bible narrows down the general geographical location of Rosh, in order to determine the identity of Rosh more specifically, we must turn to ancient history and sources outside the Bible.

A careful study of ancient history reveals that Rosh in Ezekiel's day was a group of fierce northerly people called the Sarmatians.

The Sarmatians were an Iranian tribe of nomadic people that inhabited the area around the Caspian Sea from the time of about 900 B.C. The Sarmatians were known by the Assyrians as the *Ras* or *Rashu.* An ancient Assyrian inscription written about 700 B.C. refers to an attack upon the Rashu of the land of Rashu. The land of Rashu was on the northern border of ancient Elam in the area between the Black and Caspian Seas. The Hebrew spelling of Rosh presupposes an earlier pronunciation as Rash, a form that agrees closely with the one used by the Assyrians.

Another ancient inscription refers to the ancient people of Rosh or the Sarmatians. *The Babylonian Chronicle* in 613-12 B.C. refers to the land of Rasapu. During a northern campaign by the Babylonian king Nabopolassar, he went into the area of Nisibin and spoils and prisoners from the land of Rasapu were brought before him at Nineveh. The area of Rasapu, like the land of Rashu of the Assyrians, is located in Sarmatia, the area around the Caucasus Mountains between the Black and Caspian Seas. Herodotus confirms this location because he frequently mentions the "Sauromatians" in Book Four of his *Histories* in connection with military campaigns against Cyrus and the Scythians in about 540 B.C. He locates Sauromatia between the Black and Caspian Seas just north of the Caucasus Mountains. This area today is occupied by the former Soviet republics of Armenia, Georgia, and Azerbaijan.

Another important link between the ancient Sarmatians and Rosh is found in the word *Rus*. George Vernadsky, the most noted scholar on Russian history in the world, has written several volumes on Russian history and has written extensively on the origin of the word Rus, which all agree later became the name Russia. He believes that the word Rus which later became Russia is of Iranian origin and refers to the ancient Sarmatians. Many other scholars agree with him in this identification.

Gesenius, the Hebrew scholar, says that Rosh is *"undoubtedly the Russians, who are mentioned by the Byzantine writers of the tenth century, under the name Ros, dwelling to the north of Taurus. . . as dwelling on the river Rha (Wolga). "*

Rus was also the name of the great Kievan Empire (A.D. 862). Eventually, the name Ros or Rus became the name of the entire area of modern Russia when the Latin suffix "ia" was added somewhere in the sixteenth century. Therefore, it is clear from ancient history that Rosh is Russia! The ancient people of Rosh inhabited the former southern republics of the U.S.S.R. and the former Russian republic. Therefore, we know that these parts of the former Soviet Union are included in the great Gog coalition in Ezekiel 38-39. The mention of Rosh clearly shows us that one of Gog's allies in this invasion will be Russia.

Many have thought that the fall of the Soviet Union totally eliminated Russia from the prophetic picture. However, the fall of the Soviet Union and the rise of the independent Moslem republics may actually give Russia a stronger alliance and stake in Islamic affairs.

The Jerusalem Post, May 21, 1992, reports:

> *"What the West seems to have forgotten is that Russian interest in the Middle East precedes the advent of communism. It is not about to disappear with the demise of the Soviet empire. In fact, Russia has certain advantages in the regional power play. Communism's sweet promise may have lost its appeal for the region's oppressed peoples. But the rise of independent Islamic republics within the Russian orbit may become a far more effective weapon in the battle for their hearts and minds."*

Moreover, Russia now has a military assistance treaty with Iran and has supplied Iran with twenty to thirty MiG-29 fighters and two kilo class submarines. Keep your eyes on the Islamic world, but don't count the Russians out. When Gog and his allies invade Israel, the Russians will be there with her!

Meshech and Tubal

Students of Bible prophecy have consistently identified Meshech and Tubal with the Russian cities of Moscow and Tobolsk. However, this identification is based on similarity of sound and pronunciation rather than solid historical evidence. Meshech and Tubal are identified in ancient history with the Mushki and Tabal of the Assyrians and the Moschi and Tibareni of the Greeks who inhabited territory that is in the modern nation of Turkey. At every point in the history of these two nations, they occupied territory that is presently in the modern nation of Turkey.

Gomer

Gomer has been commonly identified generally as the nations of Eastern Europe and more specifically as Germany. However, ancient history clearly identifies biblical Gomer with the Akkadian *Gi-mir-ra-a*, the Armenian *Gamir*, the Assyrian *Gimirrai*, and the Greek *Kimmerioi* or *Cimmerians*.

This group of people originally lived in the area of Southern Russia just north of the Black Sea. However, in 700 B.C. the Cimmerians were driven into the area of modern Turkey by the Scythians. The descendants of Gomer still inhabited this area as late as the first century A.D. Josephus says that the Galatians, who were located in central Turkey, were called Gomerites.

Togarmah

Ancient Togarmah is also found in the territory of the modern nation of Turkey. Togarmah was known variously as *Tegarma*, *Tagarma*, *Takarama*, and *Til-garimmu*. While scholars disagree slightly on the exact location of Togarmah, it is always associated with a city or district within the boundaries of the modern nation of Turkey. Therefore, it is clear that Turkey will be one of the major players in this last days invasion. Turkey is busy today developing alliances with the five new Moslem nations in Central Asia that inhabit the territory of ancient Magog. Turkey is represented by the nations of Meshech, Tubal, Gomer, and Togarmah, and Central Asia is Magog, and these nations are forming close ties to one another just as Ezekiel predicted in 570 B.C.

Persia

The first word in Ezekiel 38:5 is ''Persia.'' The ancient

Persian Empire occupied center stage in the world for two hundred years from 539 B.C. to 331 B.C. Today, however, Persia, the modern nation of Iran, is once again a focus of world attention. Iran is the most militant, radical, fundamentalist Moslem nation in the world. With the devastation of Iraq's military machine in the Persian Gulf war, Iran has now emerged as the most formidable foe in the Middle East-Persian Gulf region. Iran is now considered by experts to be ''Israel's New Public Enemy Number One.''

Iran is amassing a military arsenal at an alarming rate. As already mentioned, Iran has purchased fighters and submarines from Russia. Iran is currently spending $2 billion a year on conventional arms. Iran has a new five-year, $3 billion deal with North Korea to purchase one hundred and fifty No-Dong I missiles with a range of six hundred and twenty-five miles and a one thousand, seven hundred and sixty-pound conventional payload. This new missile will double Iran's missile range, bringing both Saudi Arabia and Israel into Iran's range. Iran is also making deals with China and Pakistan. Iran, which has its own uranium mines, recently purchased two ''civilian'' nuclear reactors from China and bomb-related technical help from Pakistan. Iran is also believed to have an unexploded U.S. Cruise missile in its possession.

Even more alarming to most experts are Iran's growing ties to Sudan in North Africa. Iran provides military and technical assistance to Sudan, and reportedly has completed a twenty-five-year pact with Sudan which gives it access to Port Sudan, an army base in the Gebait Hills on the Red Sea, four guerilla training bases to the north of Khartoum, and forward storage facilities for war material. Iran and Sudan are partners in an unholy alliance to spread *jihad*, or holy war, throughout the Middle East, Persian Gulf, and Africa. Iran is using Sudan as her launching pad for terror! This alliance for terror was predicted by Ezekiel twenty-six hundred years ago, because the next nation mentioned in Ezekiel 38:5 is the ancient nation of Cush which is modern-day Sudan.

Ethiopia (Cush)

Ancient Cush was called *Kusu* by the Assyrians and Babylonians, *Kos* or *Kas* by the Egyptians, and *Nubia* by the Greeks. Secular history locates Cush as the land directly south of ancient Egypt extending down past the modern city of Khartoum, which is the capital of the modern nation of Sudan. Bible dictionaries and encyclopedias consistently identify Cush as the region south of Egypt that is Nubia, or modern Sudan.

It is fascinating that Ezekiel the prophet wrote twenty-six hundred years ago that one of Iran's chief allies in her invasion into Israel in the last days would be Cush or Sudan. In fact these two nations are listed side by side in Ezekiel 38:5: "Persia, Ethiopia (Cush)." Iran's chief ally today is Sudan. The close alliance of these two nations is just one more strong indicator that the invasion predicted in Ezekiel 38-39 may be soon!

Libya

The nation of Libya or Put is another of Iran's allies in the last-days coalition against Israel. It is not difficult to envision Muammar Qadaffi joining with his radical, militant Moslem brothers to invade Israel in the near future.

Egypt

One more nation, not mentioned in Ezekiel 38, will participate in the great Gog invasion--the nation of Egypt. Ezekiel 38 and Daniel 11:40-42 are parallel passages. In Daniel 11:40, Daniel refers to the invading force as "the king of the south" and the "king of the north." Daniel 11:42 clearly mentions Egypt as an ally of Put (Libya) and Cush (Sudan). The mighty king of the south then is a confederacy of Moslem North African nations who will invade Israel in the last days, and Egypt will be a chief participant in this massive invasion.

In the last year, fundamentalist Islam has been plaguing the government in Egypt. *U.S. News and World Report* (7/19/93) calls the present tension in Egypt, "The battle for Egypt." Islamic militants have made it abundantly clear that they will use any means to overthrow the secular government of Hosni Mubarek. Islamic radicals are using every opportunity, including infiltrating the military, to replace Mubarek's secular government with a government based on Islamic law such as Iran and Sudan. In fact, Iran and Sudan are the two primary forces at work behind the scenes to overthrow the government. When they succeed, all of the nations mentioned in Ezekiel 38 and Daniel 11:40-42 will be in place to fulfill God's prophetic program outlined over two thousand years ago!

When Will Gog Meet God?

One of the important, yet difficult, questions to answer concerning the invasion described in Ezekiel 38 is when will it transpire? There are six main views among conservative, pre-Millennial scholars:

1. before the Tribulation period (before the Rapture);
2. near the beginning of the Tribulation;
3. near the middle of the Tribulation;
4. at the end of the Tribulation;
5. at the beginning of the Millennium; and
6. at the end of the Millennium.

While one should not be dogmatic concerning the timing of this invasion, there are three chronological indicators in Ezekiel 38 that provide help in determining the specific time of the attack.

First, according to Ezekiel 37:11-12 and 38:8 Israel must be regathered into the land before this invasion can occur. Of course, this began in 1948 and is continuing to this day.

Second, Ezekiel 38:8,11,14 reveal that Israel must be resting in her land in peace and prosperity. While this precondition has never been met in past history, the recently signed peace treaty between Yitzhak Rabin and Yasser Arafat could be a first step to the realization of peace and prosperity in Israel. Other Arab nations, such as Lebanon, Jordan, and Syria, are now lining up at the peace table to get their slice of the peace pie. One can readily see that the situation is ripe for the Antichrist to appear on the scene and broker the Middle East deal that will give Israel peace in fulfillment of Daniel 9:27.

The third chronological marker in Ezekiel 38 is the phrase "the latter years" (Ezek. 38:8) and the identical phrase "the latter days" (Ezek. 38:16). This identical terminology is used fifteen times in the Old Testament and always refers to either the Tribulation period or the Millennium; however, the majority of references are to the Tribulation period.

Taking all of these factors into account, the view that seems most probable is that the invasion will occur sometime in the first half of the Tribulation period, probably just before the mid-point, because according to the parallel passage in Daniel 11:40-42, this invasion is the proximate cause of Antichrist's invasion of Israel and establishment of his headquarters in Jerusalem (Dan. 11:41-45a).

The Great Slaughter

Gog and his allies will invade Israel in the last days with a massive, well-prepared army. Israel will be living in her land unprotected and unsuspecting. This will look like the biggest mismatch in military history. When Gog mounts this offensive, it will look like the nation of Israel is finished. It will look like Satan has finally achieved his purpose of destroying the seed of Abraham. However, God is in control of the entire situation. Gog and his allies are under God's authority and cannot go one step beyond His purposes. In fact, God is the one drawing and summoning Gog to meet his final destiny in the land of Israel.

God will orchestrate the whole situation until it appears to be utterly hopeless for Israel, then He will intervene so that He may demonstrate to the entire world that He is without equal.

When God brings Gog into the land of Israel, Gog and his forces will cover the land of Israel like a storm or a cloud covering the land (Ezek. 38:9,16). In proud, inflated confidence, Gog and his allies will move in for the kill. They will look invincible. But God will intervene on behalf of His people.

> *"And it shall come to pass at the same time when Gog shall come against the land of Israel, saith the Lord God, that my fury shall come up in my face. For in my jealousy and in the fire of my wrath have I spoken . . ."* (Ezek. 38:18-19).

Notice the words God uses--"My fury," "My anger," "My zeal," and "My blazing wrath." God will pour out his vengeance on Gog like a flood.

God will use four primary means to destroy Gog and his army. The first is a great earthquake.

> *"For in my jealousy and in the fire of my wrath have I spoken, Surely in that day there shall be a great shaking in the land of Israel; So that the fishes of the sea, and the fowls of the heaven, and the beasts of the field, and all creeping things that creep upon the earth, and all the men that are upon the face of the earth, shall shake at my presence, and the mountains shall be thrown down, and the steep places shall fall, and every wall shall fall to the ground"* (Ezek. 38:19-20).

God will send an earthquake of unparalleled strength to

the land of Israel to wipe out the invading horde.

The second means God will use to annihilate Gog will be infighting among the different troop.

> *"And I will call for a sword against him throughout all my mountains, saith the Lord God: every man's sword shall be against his brother"* (Ezek. 38:21).

Apparently, when the earthquake hits the land and the mountains are thrown down and the steep pathways collapse, Gog's army will break into chaos. His invading force which looked invincible will turn against itself. Remember, Gog's army will be made up of troops from many nations: Russia, the Moslem nations of Central Asia, Turkey, Iran, Egypt, Sudan, and Libya. When God violently shakes the land and the troops fall into confusion, they will begin to kill one another. It is likely that in anger, frustration, and confusion, the armies of each of these nations will turn against one another. Troops in this army will speak Russian, Turkic, Arabic, and Farsi. When mass confusion breaks out, soldiers will probably begin killing anyone who does not speak their language. The third means God will use to decimate Gog is pestilence or plagues.

> *"And I will plead against him with pestilence and with blood . . ."* (Ezek. 38:22).

The word used here for pestilence is used in Exodus 9:3 of the divine plague on Pharaoh's livestock. God will visit Gog and his troops with a horrible plague which will add to the misery and devastation that will already be inflicted.

The final, climatic judgment God will use to eradicate Gog's horde will be fire and brimstone from heaven.

> *". . . and I will rain upon him, and upon his*

> *bands, and upon the many people that are with*
> *him, an overflowing rain, and great hail-*
> *stones, fire, and brimstone''* (Ezek. 38:22).

Sodom and Gomorrah are two of the world's most well-known cities. These wicked cities became famous when God poured out fire and brimstone on them and blotted them out because of their heinous sin. To this day, people look for the ruins of these two cities, but God so completely wiped them out that the ruins have never been found. Just as God poured out fire and brimstone on Sodom and Gomorrah, He will devastate Gog and his allies, only on a vastly greater scale.

God will not only send fire upon the armies of Gog, but He will also pour out fire on Gog's homeland and headquarters in Magog.

> *''And I will send a fire on Magog, and among*
> *them that dwell carelessly in the isles: and they*
> *shall know that I am the Lord''* (Ezek. 39:6).

Millions of people will be wiped off the face of the earth in a moment of time! The destruction of Gog is not the end of the story. Ezekiel goes on in 39:4-24 to set forth the results or aftermath of Gog's devastation. The aftermath primarily consists of two events: the burial of the dead bodies and the feeding of the birds and beasts on the carrion.

The extent of the slaughter can be seen from the fact that it takes seven months to bury all the bodies of the slain to cleanse the land.

> *''And it shall come to pass in that day, that I*
> *will give unto Gog a place there of graves in*
> *Israel, the valley of the passengers on the east*
> *of the sea: and it shall stop the noses of the*
> *passengers: and there shall they bury Gog and*

all his multitude: and they shall call it The
valley of Hamon-gog. And seven months shall
the house of Israel be burying of them, that they
may cleanse the land'' (Ezek. 39:11-12).

The corpses will be buried east of the Dead Sea in
ancient Moab, or the modern nation of Jordan. The phrase
''those who pass by east'' is probably a proper name describing
the mountains of Abarim east of the Dead Sea. Therefore,
Gog's burial will be in ''the valley of those who pass by east''
or the Valley of Abarim across the Dead Sea.

The total number of corpses that will be gathered will
be so great that the ''valley of travelers'' will be blocked. Due
to the number of corpses, the name of the valley will be changed
to ''Hamon-gog,'' which means ''the Valley of the hordes of
Gog.'' The only piece of land Gog will claim in the land of Israel
will be his burial plot! Gog will set out to bury Israel, but God
will bury Gog! Another detail is given to emphasize the vast
proportions of the catastrophe. After the initial clean-up
operation, squads of men will be employed to search the land
for additional corpses.

''And they shall sever out men of continual
employment, passing through the land to bury
with the passengers those that remain upon the
face of the earth, to cleanse it: after the end of
seven months shall they search. And the pas-
sengers that pass through the land, when any
seeth a man's bone, then shall he set up a sign
by it, till the buriers have buried it in the valley
of Hamon-gog. And also the name of the city
shall be Ha-mo-nah. Thus shall they cleanse
the land'' (Ezek. 39:14-16).

As these clean-up squads go through the land, they will

set up markers wherever they see a human bone. When the gravediggers come through the land, they will see the markers and take the remains to the Valley of Hamon-gog for burial. The cleansing operation will be so extensive that a town will be established in the valley at the gravesites to aid those who are cleansing the land. The name of the town is "Hamonah," which is a form of the word "hordes."

The second result of the destruction of Gog is even more horrible and gruesome than the massive burial operation. The carnage that results from the slaughter will provide a great feast for the birds of the air and the beasts of the field. God refers to the carnage as "My sacrifice," and "My table," to which he invites the birds and the beasts as His guests.

> *"Thou shalt fall upon the mountains of Israel, thou, and all thy bands, and the people that is with thee: I will give thee unto the ravenous birds of every sort, and to the beasts of the field to be devoured. Thou shalt fall upon the open field: for I have spoken it, saith the Lord God. . . . And, thou son of man, thus saith the Lord God; Speak unto every feathered fowl, and to every beast of the field, Assemble yourselves, and come; gather yourselves on every side to my sacrifice that I do sacrifice for you, even a great sacrifice upon the mountains of Israel, that ye may eat flesh, and drink blood. Ye shall eat the flesh of the mighty, and drink the blood of the princes of the earth, of rams, of lambs, and of goats, of bullocks, all of them fatlings of Bashan. And ye shall eat fat till ye be full, and drink blood till ye be drunken, of my sacrifice which I have sacrificed for you. Thus ye shall be filled at my table with horses and chariots, with mighty men, and with all men of war, saith*

the Lord God'' (Ezek. 39:4-5,17-20).

A similar scene is pictured in Revelation 19:17-18 after the final battle of this age at Armageddon:

> *''And I saw an angel standing in the sun; and he cried with a loud voice, saying to all the fowls that fly in the midst of heaven, Come and gather yourselves together unto the supper of the great God; That ye may eat the flesh of kings, and the flesh of captains, and the flesh of mighty men, and the flesh of horses, and of them that sit on them, and the flesh of all men, both free and bond, both small and great.''*

This is the ultimate humiliation and degradation for proud human rulers. Both Gog and his army, and then later the Antichrist in Revelation 19, will be slaughtered by God and given as sacrifices to the animals and birds. Daniel 4:37 says of God, ''. . . those that walk in pride he is able to abase.'' He alone is God and He will not give His glory to another!

Conclusion

Ezekiel 38-39 clearly predicts a great invasion of Israel in the last days by a vast horde of nations. The dissolution of the Soviet Union, rather than annulling this great prophecy, has made its fulfillment more certain and imminent than at any time in history. The fall of the Soviet Union has spawned the creation of six, new independent Moslem nations that reside in the ancient land of Magog, and has paved the way for the meteoric rise of fundamentalist, radical, militant Islam in the Middle East-Persian Gulf region.

A careful examination of the names in Ezekiel 38:1-6 reveals that eleven primary nations will be involved in this invasion: Russia, Turkey, the five Moslem nations of Central

Asia, Iran, Libya, Sudan, and Egypt. All of these nations, except Russia, are Moslem, and all are either already militant Moslem or have the seeds of radicalism at work. It is easy to foresee the nations mentioned in the passage coming together in the near future to invade Israel.

Ezekiel is clear that when these nations do descend upon regathered, resting Israel, they will meet their demise on the mountains of Israel. The destruction of Gog and his allies is the trigger that plunges the world into the Great Tribulation and moves the Antichrist to invade Israel and begin his three-and-a-half year reign of terror.

What a privilege is ours to live in days like these when we can witness the unfolding of God's prophetic program for this world!

Maranatha!

Chapter Eight

Satan's Final Assault

I.D.E. Thomas

Importance of 1948

For most Christians, probably 1948 was the most momentous year since Pentecost in Jerusalem, nearly two thousand years ago. Six amazing distinctives apply to that year.

1. **For better or worse, the National Council of Churches was founded** with the hope that one day it would usher in a one-world church. The hope was that by uniting many churches, problems would disappear. Personally I cannot see that by uniting two dead churches you can get one live one. Uniting cemeteries will not lead to a resurrection!

2. **The European Common Market** came into being at the Hague Congress. A strong unified Europe seems to get closer each year. Some interpret this as a revived Roman Empire.

3. **The re-establishment of the state of Israel:** When David Ben Gurion banged the table in Tel Aviv at 4:00 p.m. on May 14, 1948, he proclaimed for the world to hear: *"The establishment of the Jewish state called Israel."* Then he added: *"The Bible is our mandate."* Eleven minutes later, the president of the U.S.A. recognized the state of Israel. He was Harry Truman. His swift action helped his re-election later that year.

4. **The discovery of the Dead Sea Scrolls**, November 1947, became known to the world in 1948. They contain some amazing documents.

   Punch magazine of London offered a prize for the shortest poem submitted. This was the poem that won:

   > *How odd*
   > *Of God*
   > *To choose*
   > *The Jews*

   The month there was another short poem:

   > *Oh no*
   > *'Tis not*
   > *God knows*
   > *What's whot!*

   It is still claimed that the IQ of a Jewish child is consistently higher than that of a non-Jewish child. Why? One interesting answer given is this: for hundreds of years in our Western world, the most intelligent and talented young men went into the Church for their career. The Church offered them the only career in which intellectual ability was rewarded, regardless of the origin of the young man. But the priesthood exacted a price—celibacy. It meant that the most intelligent portion of the population had no offspring. Their genes were siphoned off, as generation after generation went into the Church. With the Jews, the priesthood also attracted the most ambitious students, and they became rabbis. But they were allowed, indeed encouraged, to marry and have children. They followed the injunction of Scripture to be fruitful. Although not conscious of this, Jewish breeding was *for* intelligence, Gentile breeding *against*.

5. **The Space Age began**: In 1948 experiments with liquid hydrogen proved that a rocket could be sent into space beyond the Earth's gravitational pull.

6. **When men were beginning to go into space, strange objects from space began appearing on earth.** The modern rash of UFO sightings began in 1947-48. Kenneth Arnold was piloting his plane through the crystal clear skies around the Cascade mountains in the state of Washington. He saw nine crescent-shaped discs, and said that they were "like saucers skipping across the water." Soon the word "flying saucer" entered our vocabulary. Since then flying saucers have been seen by millions in the U.S. alone, plus millions and millions more in countries all over the globe. They have been seen by unknown, insignificant, run-of-the-mill people, and by famous celebrities including two former presidents—Carter and Reagan. Nearly fifty years have passed since then, and the UFO mystery has survived countless criticisms and endless denials. And we certainly know more today in 1993 than we did fifty years ago. In yet another fifty years men will know far more facts and figures than the inkling we know today. *Make no mistake, the UFOs have come to stay.*

In view of all this, is there any biblical evidence that can shed light on this very perplex question?

Jesus, whilst on earth, made a statement that most scholars and prophets have completely neglected. This is why Christians today are completely mystified by all that they hear about strange beings from space arriving on our planet. They think it is all fantasy and has nothing to do with fact.

Let me quote to you what Jesus said: *"But as the days of Noe were, so also shall the coming of the Son of man be"* (Matt. 24:37). We have spent our time describing the end days as days of earthquakes, floods, fires, famines, wars, rumors of wars. . . . And yet we have always had these. However, one thing did happen in the days of Noah that has never been repeated since, but will be repeated at the end of time. Noah who belongs to the beginning of time, tells us of what to expect at the end of time. *Noah is the key figure in the Bible as to the end of time.*

What happened in the days of Noah? A vital question because the closing scenes of our age will be a reproduction of what happened then. What did happen?

- *There was a tendency then, as now, to worship God as Elohim,* that is the Creator and Benefactor, not as *Jehovah,* the God of mercy.
- *A rapid progress in arts, education, and knowledge.*
- *A vast increase of population.*
- *The rejection of the preaching of God's servants, Enoch and Noah* (Noah preached for one hundred and twenty years.
- *The appearance upon earth of beings from space,* and their unlawful sexual conduct with women of the human race. This was one of the most awesome characteristics of the days of Noah. This event has not startled any age except our age today. Things that ruined the ancient world, are already appearing in our age today. If you diligently study the book of Genesis, and the life of Noah, and compare it with what is now happening in our time, you will soon realize we are on the edge of the precipice. *Not only are UFOs here, but here also are the space beings who travel in them.*

Extra-Biblical Evidence

I am not going to choose evidence that is contra-biblical, but pro-biblical.

In 1947 an Arab boy tending his sheep accidentally discovered an ancient cave near the Dead Sea. In it was a priceless collection of ancient scrolls—the Dead Sea Scrolls or Qumran Texts. Among these texts was one known as *The Genesis Apocryphon.*

At first they thought it was the long lost book of Lamech, but it was not. The scroll, however, does contain a speech by Lamech. Lamech was the son of Methuselah and the father of Noah, the ninth of the ten patriarchs of the antediluvian world.

The *Genesis Apocryphon* mentions the Nephilim, and makes specific reference to the sons of God and the daughters of men. It elaborates considerably on the succinct statement found in the Bible, in Genesis 6, and provides many valuable insights.

Unfortunately, the scroll found in 1947 had been much mutilated by the ravages of time and humidity. The sheets were badly stuck together, and it took many years to decipher the text. When finally it was made public, the document confirmed that celestial beings from space had landed on planet earth. More than that, it told how these beings had mated with earth women and begot giants.

The story of Lamech is highly interesting. He had been away from home on a long journey. When he finally returned, he discovered to his chagrin that his wife, Bat-Enosh, had given birth to a baby boy in his absence. He was sure that the child had not been sired by him, and what is more, the child bore no resemblance to him or to anyone in his family. Adding to the mystery was the fact that the boy was extremely beautiful, and when he opened his eyes the whole house would light up. Lamech said: "*. . . he is not sprung from me but from the angels.*"

Lamech did what most husbands would do: he re-proached his wife for infidelity. Bat-Enosh, however, swore by all that was sacred to her that Lamech himself must have sired the child. She had not known any other man, not a stranger—and note this—not a *watcher* or *heavenly being.*

Lamech must have realized, in spite of the protestations of his wife, that the child could have been conceived by one of these heavenly beings. If that were the case, the child belonged to the Nephilim.

To try to solve this mystery, Lamech sought the advice of his father, Methuselah. When he heard the story, Methuselah immediately went to his own father, the wise and godly Enoch. The family's reputation was at stake and something had to be done.

Enoch, whose name means ''*the intelligent,*'' or ''*the learned,*'' sensed what had happened. He sent his son back with the disturbing news that the earth would soon be visited by a terrible catastrophe and judgment.

Clearly, the human race was in grave danger. But as for the little boy, whose birth remained a mystery, Enoch advised Lamech to raise him as his own child, and that he should be called *Noah*. Noah had been specially chosen by God to survive the coming judgment, and should be the progenitor of the new inhabitants of planet earth.

Although Noah could not have been of the Nephilim, it is obvious that strange things were happening on the earth at that time.

These extra-biblical documents should not be placed on par with the Scriptures. However, when they corroborate the Scriptures we can safely take their evidence as true.

The Book of Enoch

This was an ancient best-seller, and a best-seller in the days of Christ. It was widely read and discussed, and its impact was tremendous. Without question it was the most notable apocalyptic work outside the canonical Scriptures. R.H.C. Charles (an authority in this field) tells us that *"the influence of I Enoch on the N.T. has been greater than that of all the other apocryphal and pseudepigraphical books put together."*

Yet this Book of Enoch was unknown in Europe until the eighteenth century. It was discovered by James Bruce in 1773.

There are actually three Books of Enoch: *I Enoch* (known as the "Ethiopic Enoch"); *II Enoch* (Slavonic Enoch); and *III Enoch* (Hebrew Enoch). I Enoch is the important one. In some copies of the Ethiopic Bible it is not only included in the canon, but is the first book in the Bible, preceding even Genesis.

This Book of Enoch in some ways prepared the way for Christian doctrine. From this book also the Manual of Discipline (Qumran) received its solar calendar. *Tertullian and some of the early Church fathers included it as part of the canon. Jude the apostle regarded it as inspired Scripture, and quoted it.*

Who was the author? The Enoch of the Bible was one of the outstanding characters of Scripture, although he receives only four verses in the whole Bible (two in the Old Testament and two in the New Testament)! He was the seventh of the ten patriarchs between Adam and Noah. He was known for his exceptional piety and godliness. The Book of Enoch adds that he will return to earth at the end of time, and will be one of the two witnesses to be martyred on the streets of Jerusalem. Most scholars, however, claim that the biblical Enoch could not be the author of this book that bears his name. They suggest a later author compiled the work, using a number of different sources. By using Enoch's name it guaranteed the book's popularity. The biblical Enoch, however, could have been one of these important sources.

What does the Bible of Enoch tell us? Enoch obviously had access to classified information way beyond the reach of mortal man. Much of this information is couched in allegorical and symbolic language, and the meaning frequently escapes us. But beneath the abstruse verbal foliage there lies some amazing data.

Among other things, it tells of the bizarre event referred to in *Genesis 6*. And it contributes a number of detailed particulars not found in the Genesis record.

- Enoch describes his visit to the fifth heaven, where he saw giants with withered faces. He calls them the *gregori* or *fallen angels*. They were the ones who had broken their vows and married the daughters of men, and had *"befouled the earth with their deeds."*
- Enoch also mentions that *"giants were born and marvelous big men and great enmity."*
- Like the book of Daniel, he calls them *watchers* or *sons of God.*
- They descended to the earth in *the days of Jared*, the father of Enoch (Gen. 5:18). There is an American organization called "The Sons of Jared." Their publication is called *The Jaredite Advocate*. The aim of this group is to declare war on all the descendants of the watchers, including notorious kings and dictators who have tyrannized mankind—sort of a celestial Mafia!
- These watchers instructed the people of earth in many studies: charms and enchantments, magic, the cosmetic trade. . . . Tertullian asks with astringency why should the angels have to instruct the women of earth in the cosmetic arts?! If they had succeeded in charming angels without such aids, it should be an easy matter to charm

men!

Another study was astrology, and a highly interesting one: the art of fashioning weapons. Comyns Beaumont adds ammunition and explosives.

■ *It confirms the Genesis record of the depraved state of mankind at the time; the coming of the Nephilim; and the birth of the giants.* And also this significant addition: *they disclosed certain secrets, eternal secrets (classified material), which God did not intend for fallen man to possess.*

■ The Book of Enoch also reveals how this information from pre-diluvian times was preserved for succeeding generations. Enoch wrote it all down, and gave it to his son Methuselah to preserve. The book could have been preserved in the ark with Noah, or buried deep in the earth—as indicated by the Assyrian version of the flood.

The Book of Jubilee

This book adds a few more details. It suggests a date: 461 Annus Mundi. According to Bishop Ussher's calculation, this would be 3543 B.C. It also underscores the point that the Nephilim were associated with Jared, the fifth in line from Adam.

Other ancient documents that refer to the Nephilim are: *The Zadokite Document, The Apocalypse of Baruch, The Testament of the Twelve Patriarchs. . . .*

Folklore, Fables, and Myths

There is an abundance of these that tell of giants upon the earth in ancient times; and also of sexual union between *demi-gods from heaven and women from earth. Modern, specialized research tells us that many of these myths emerged from a kernel of historic fact.*

Andrew Tomas states that mythology and folklore are *"thought-fossils depicting the story of vanished cultures in symbols and allegories."*

> *"More and more we are finding that mythology in general though greatly contorted very often has some historical base. And the interesting thing is that **one myth which occurs over and over again in many parts of the world is that somewhere a long time ago supernatural beings had sexual intercourse with natural women and produced a special breed of people.**"* (Francis S. Schaeffer)

Most people are acquainted with the mythologies of ancient Greece and Rome. The gods and semi-gods in these traditions go under different names, but their behavior has a common denominator. Whether you call them Zeus or Jupiter, Aphrodite or Venus, Eros or Cupid . . . they share the same sex-orgies and promiscuities. And their offspring are similar. *The heroes of ancient Greece were spawned " by divine fathers and human mothers. One of them was Hercules." The amorous escapades of Zeus illustrate the actions of uncontrolled spirit-beings lusting after flesh.*

> *"The whole story of Greek mythology is an expanded version of that astonishing verse in the Bible: 'The sons of God saw the daughters of men that they were fair; and took them wives of all they chose.'"* (Emil Gaverluk)

Such mythologies are not limited to Greece and Rome. *Erick von Daniken* (not known for his theological orthodoxy, but a compiler of some amazing facts) supplies a wealth of material from all over the world, that tell the same kind of stories in other cultures and histories.

Tie all these together, and you will be amazed by their common core. *With only slight variation, these all tell us of the traffic between the "sons of God" and the "daughters of men"; their sexual activities; and their unusual offspring.* And these myths belong to people who were far removed from each other as regards time, space, and language. This means that collaboration was out of the question. It is a truly amazing phenomenon. How does one explain it?

Could it be that at some distant point in time, these bizarre events actually did take place? *Rather than being the fertile product of the imagination of primitive man, they were instead man's crude description of what actually happened.* With time, of course, these developed an overgrowth of fictional imagery and imaginative fantasy . . . but beneath that overgrowth lay the planet of truth. *What began as history ended up as legend. What began as fact developed into fable.*

From all the documents we have, it is obvious that these space beings—although they fall short of omnipotence—had great power, far greater power than normal human beings. The Bible designates one of them as *"prince of this world."* When one recalls the havoc they have caused the individuals, and the demonic influence they have exercised on certain nations and certain leaders resulting in the massacre of millions . . . one knows that they are not beings from this earth. They are beings from space, and demonic in character.

Stalin once said, *"To kill one is a tragedy; to kill a million a statistic."*

No one denies the power of demonic beings; but it is vital to realize their whole purpose as they enter our planet. Their chief purpose is nothing less than to thwart God's plan of redemption. This has been their major target from the beginning: *to destroy the Royal Seed, and thus deprive man of* his rightful place in God's kingdom.

As to the future, the Bible predicts that before Christ's return, these spirit-beings that were seen in Genesis 6, will return in a final, concerted attempt to seduce the human race. "But as the days of Noe were, so shall the coming of the Son of man be." Their human agent will be Antichrist, "whose coming is after the working of Satan" (2 Thess. 2:9).

Could there be a linkage between the return of these extraterrestrials and the cryptic word found in Daniel 2:43? "And... they shall mingle themselves with the seed of men: but they shall not cleave one to another, even as iron is not mixed with clay."

Is it feasible that those who are entering our atmosphere today, under the guise of space beings, and traveling in mysterious space vehicles, are the same demonic agencies? Is this the first phase of their planned return?

Jaques Vallee does not use biblical terminology, nor does he write from the standpoint of Scripture, nevertheless he comes surprisingly close to the conclusion of Scripture.

> "The experience of a close encounter with a UFO is a shattering physical and mental ordeal. The trauma has effects that go far beyond what the witnesses recall consciously. New types of behavior are conditioned, and new types of beliefs are promoted. The social, political, and religious consequences of the experience are enormous if they are considered, not in the days or weeks following the sighting, but over the timespan of a generation. Could it be that such effects are actually intended, through some process of social conditioning? Could it be that both the believers and the skeptics are being manipulated by what I jokingly call the Higher Intelligence

*Agency? Is the public being deceived and led
to false conclusions by someone who is using
the UFO witnesses to propagate revolutionary
new ideas?''*

No one but a being like Satan could fill such position.
Two thousand years ago, the Apostle Paul warned his readers
of this very thing. He told of the coming of Antichrist to the
world scene, masterminded by Satan himself. His work, says
Paul, would be characterized by *''. . . power and signs and lying
wonders, And with all deceivableness of unrighteousness in
them that perish . . .''* (2 Thess. 2:9-10).

*This is the ''social conditioning'' in which these alien
beings are engaged. It is to delude and deceive the human
race. Christ issued the same warning:*

*''And then if any man shall say to you, Lo, here
is Christ; or, lo, he is there; believe him not:
For false Christs and false prophets shall rise,
and shall shew signs and wonders, to seduce,
if it were possible, even the very elect''* (Mark
13:21-22).

For their strategy to succeed, these agencies will have
to be extremely cunning. They will have to attack with *''lim-
itless deceit''* (Berkeley version of 2 Thess. 2:10). Posing as
our friends and allies, they will convince people that they were
sent here to save us. Humans will experience as never before
''the wiles of the devil.''

Again and again the Bible urges us not to be ignorant.
There is no defense against demonic deception *but a thorough
acquaintance with the truth.* Jesse Penn Lewis made a pro-
found statement:

''Since deception is based on ignorance, and

*not on the moral character, a Christian is 'true' and 'faithful' up to the knowledge he has, must be open to deception in the sphere where he is ignorant of the 'devices' of the devil, (2 Cor. 2:11) and what he is able to do. A 'true' and 'faithful' Christian is liable to be deceived by the devil because of his **ignorance.***"

To achieve his power, the devil has to control the mind. It is there that the battle is joined. *The devil confuses the mind (2 Thess. 2:2); he diverts the mind (James 4:8); he discourages the mind (Heb. 12:3).*

*The bottom line: How can infinite man withstand, let alone repel, such an invasion? The answer in one is: **Christ**.* His Name and His authority are the only resources we have to repel such entities. He commanded the demons when here on earth, and *each time they obeyed. Repeat: each time they obeyed.* No recorded exception! This was the wonder of His power that even His own enemies had to admit: *". . . for with authority commandeth he even the unclean spirits, and they do obey him"* (Mark 1:27).

Note this statement by C.S. Lewis:

"Devil is the opposite of angel only as bad man is the opposite of good man. Satan, the dictator of devils, is the opposite, not of God, but of Michael."

Don't compare Christ with Satan. Compare Satan with an angel or archangel if you will, but not with the Holy Trinity.

The future belongs to Christ. He is King over all kings, and over all dominions, powers, and principalities. Let His enemies be terrestrial or extraterrestrial, He is still Lord of lords and King of kings.

At no time is the future in doubt. We have advance information on how the battle will end. As a matter of fact *we are given a preview of tomorrow's headlines: ". . . The kingdoms of this world are become the kingdoms of our Lord, and of his Christ; and he shall reign for ever and ever"* (Rev. 11:15).

Two Cosmic Riddles

1. **At the beginning of human history there was a period of vast expertise and knowledge.** It was not the case of primitive savages roaming wild and naked in the bush. Rather, one finds men planning the pyramids, building Babylon, engineering Stonehenge, and structuring the Mayan Caracol. According to one author, it was *"climax at the beginning."*

■ A thousand years before *Darwin* (cf. *Thomas Bridges and Tierra del Fuego*) formed his theory of evolution, ancient Mayans and Toltecs carved their own version in stone. These people had a calendar more precise than ours today; they knew and used penicillin; and like the ancient Egyptians they designed great cities and mammoth pyramids. From where did they get their expertise?

■ Why did the Assyrians, who lived more than *two thousand years* before Christ, encircle the planet Saturn with *a ring of serpents?* How did they know of such rings? No other planet was depicted in that way. In addition, they recorded the different phases of the moon with an accuracy not seen again until the seventeenth century, A.D. They did it in 1400 B.C.

■ How did the ancient *Greeks* know that there were *seven* stars in Pleiades? They could only see six! Did some higher intelligence inform them?

■ The pre-Inca mountaineers of *Peru* performed amputations, bone transplants, cauterization, brain surgeries, and a variety of other complicated operations. From whom did they learn their advanced surgical skills?

■ From whom did the builders of the awesome structures of Tiahuanaco gain their knowledge *thirty* centuries ago? To erect such massive monoliths would require one hundred thousand people, unless they possessed some colossal power-cranes or mastered the secret of levitation. Those titanic blocks, some weighing fifty tons and more, were so precisely cut and interlocked that no mortar was needed to bind them. Even today you cannot pound a chisel between them. How on earth could they have done it? With nothing we know of on earth.

■ Visitors to the megaliths of Stonehenge have been mystified by a dozen riddles. How could men wearing skins have designed this computer in stone?

■ And the greatest riddle of all: where did the ancient Egyptians learn the secret of *pyramid building*? Sir Flinders Petrie called the Pyramid of Cheops *"the greatest and most accurate structure the world has ever seen."* The *Encyclopaedia Britannica*, with typical British understatement, says that the *"brain power to which it testifies is as great as that of any modern man."* The truth is: no one today could construct such a pyramid. A Japanese firm attempted the task a few years ago, and like others before them, the project ended in failure.

The exceptional structure of the first pyramid reveals knowledge of astronomical truth which is on a level with the most advanced statements of modern science.

The Great Pyramid is undoubtedly the greatest of the Seven Wonders of the World. Practically everything about it is awesome. The length of each side of the base is 365.2442 cubits—exactly the number of days in the solar year, including the extra day each four years!

The gradient of the pyramid is ten to nine. For every ten feet you ascend, you rise in altitude nine feet. Multiply the altitude of the pyramid by ten, raised to the ninth power, and you have 91,840,000 miles. The exact distance from the earth to the sun! It also means that 1,000 million pyramids would reach the sun! The Great Pyramid is full of such amazing measurements.

The riddle remains unanswered, how could the designers of this pyramid have observed the stars for twenty-two hundred years? And how could they have computed five thousand years ago, the circumference of our planet? *And how did they know the existence of a leap year every four years? This information did not become part of our store of knowledge until six hundred years ago. The pyramid builder knew it four thousand years earlier!*

One wonders whether the prophet Isaiah had this pyramid in mind when he said: *"In that day shall there be an altar to the Lord in the midst of the land of Egypt, and a pillar at the border thereof to the Lord. And it shall be for a sign and for a witness . . ."* (Isa. 19:19-20).

("In the midst" and "at the border"? Egypt used to be divided into two kingdoms: Upper and Lower Egypt. The Nile is one of the very few rivers that flows northwards. Memphis was on the border of the two Egypts. Then the Pharaoh of one Egyptian kingdom married the queen of the other, and united Egypt. Now, Memphis that used to be on the border, was in the center.)

The mystery persists. How were those mammoth blocks of stone, some seventy tons in weight, cut, polished, and finally elevated and made to fit perfectly into place? *In all, the Great Pyramid has two million blocks of stone—enough to build a six-foot wall from Los Angeles to New York.*

It is generally believed that the other pyramids **were** *occult temples or burial chambers.* Their walls **were** covered with half-human, half-animal creatures. The Pharaohs were buried inside.

But the *Great Pyramid of Cheops is different: there are no inscriptions on its walls, and no demonic symbols. What is more, its secret chambers have never been penetrated.* The Japanese have tried modern x-rays and specialized technological means to penetrate the chamber, but have failed. There is something very mysterious that keeps their x-rays from penetrating, when according to modern science it should work!

Is it almost a mere coincidence that the Great Pyramid has a missing capstone? Just like the pyramid on the reverse side of the American dollar bill. The capstone is the final stone on top of a pyramid. It is identical to the shape of the pyramid itself. Jesus Christ is referred to in the Bible as the **cornerstone**. All structures have four cornerstones, but a pyramid has five—four in the bottom corners and one on top, the capstone.

Revelation 21:16 gives a description of God's great city. Its length, breadth, and height are all equal. The very dimensions of a pyramid.

There are many more such mysteries that remain unexplained. How does one account for this awesome display of knowledge by our pre-historic ancestors? Where is the key to such cosmic riddles?

One historic author (Berosus) tells of an antediluvian *"town of books"* in *ancient Babylon.* And in the Chaldean account Noah was told to bury his books before the deluge, and to disentomb them after his "descent from the ark." Four other towns are named that contained well-known libraries—Erech, Ur, Cutha, and Larsa.

We agree with Pember when he says that we are compelled to admit that the antediluvians *"may have attained to a perfection in civilization and high culture which has scarcely yet been recovered."*

2. **The failure of science to supply an answer.**

■ A thousand years ago, men believed *the world was flat.*

Gibraltar: "Ne plus Ultra." They were wrong.

■ Five hundred years ago, *men believed the earth was the center of the universe.* Sun, moon, and stars circled the earth, rising in the east and setting in the west. We still use that terminology. Then came Nicolaus Copernicus, the Prussian astronomer, and proved that men before him had all been wrong.

■ Two hundred years ago, the famous Lavoiser with a committee of the French Academy *decided it was impossible for stones to fall from the sky.* So meteorites were described as mere stones on earth that had been struck by lightning.

■ One hundred years ago, just after *Thomas Edison* had invented his carbon filament lamp, *a Parliamentary committee* was set up in England to report on the matter. The chairman, Sir William Preece, announced the group's findings to the House of Commons: *"Electric light in the home is fanciful and absurd."*

■ Less than fifty years ago, Sir Harold Spencer Jones, director of Greenwich Observatory, announced that *man would never set foot on the surface of the moon.* In July 1969, Neil Armstrong proved him wrong.

■ Twenty-five years ago, Dr. Richard Woolley, Britain's astronomer royal, said that *"space travel is utter binge."* American and Russian astronauts have proved the astronomer royal to be royally wrong.

■ *Less than twenty-five years ago, men believed that the stories circulating about UFOs circling our globe and landing on our planet, were all hoaxes and hallucinations.* Today, more than fifteen million adult witnesses, equipped with photographs (movies and stills), physical documentation, and scientific data, have proved again that men can be wrong.

These two factors remain with us: the display of vast

knowledge and expertise at the beginning of human history, and the failure of scientific thought to supply an answer.

In my studies of demonology and Ufology, I believe that I have found the answer. What is far more important is that my answer carries biblical warrant. *Jesus before He left this earth, told us that if we are to understand the end time, go back to Genesis, and to a man called Noah. "But as in the days of Noe were, so shall also the coming of the Son of man be."*

Biblical Evidence

When human reason fails, divine revelation comes to the rescue. The key to the whole mystery is found in the Bible. Back in Genesis 6:1-2,4 we find:

> *"And it came to pass, when men began to multiply on the face of the earth, and daughters were born unto them, That the sons of God saw the daughters of men that they were fair; and they took them wives of all which they chose. . . . . There were giants in the earth in those days; and also after that, when the sons of God came in unto the daughters of men, and they bare children to them, the same became mighty men which were of old, men of renown."*

Controversy surrounds the interpretation of this passage. Strong biblical evidence, however, indicates that it refers to the bizarre union between extraterrestrials and the women of earth. *The Nephilim* were the super-human offspring of this union, and appeared on the planet before the great flood. In fact, their existence and vile corruption was the main reason for the flood. They were destroyed along with the rest of mankind. Only Noah and his family escaped their contamination and hence were saved.

Centuries later, the Nephilim emerged again, this time

on a more limited scale in the land of Canaan (Num. 13:2,25-33). As before, God ordered their annihilation.

"*Sons of God,*" and "*daughters of men,*" what sort of beings were these? Were they human or did they belong to an alien species from outer space?

There is no problem in identifying the "daughters of men." This was a familiar method of designating women in the Bible. The problem lies with the "sons of God." Three major interpretations are offered:

1. *A group within orthodox Judaism theorized that "sons of God" meant "nobles" or "magnates."* Hardly anyone accepts this view today.

2. *The vast majority of scholars and commentators today contend that "sons of God" are male descendants of Seth; and the "daughters of men" are the female descendants of Cain.* They tell us that what actually happened in Genesis 6 was an early example of *believers marrying unbelievers.* The good sons of Seth married the bad daughters of Cain, and the result of these mixed marriages was a mongrel offspring.

   Even the great Matthew Henry presented the same view: *"The sons of Seth (that is, the professors of religion) married the daughters of men, that is, those that were profane, and strangers to God and godliness. The posterity of Seth did not keep to themselves, as they ought to have done. They intermingled themselves with the excommunicated race of Cain."*

   In spite of the excellent pedigree of some of the proponents of this theory, their

argument is not convincing. Their interpretation is pure *eisegesis*--they are guilty of
reading into the text what is obviously not in
the text.
3. *The early Church fathers and early Jewish
rabbis interpreted the "sons of God" as
fallen angels.* This is my personal belief, and
that for a large number of reasons--at least
seventeen reasons.

I know that many modern Bible commentators reject
this theory, and that on *psychological* grounds. They ask how
it is possible to believe that angels from heaven could engage
in sexual relations with women from earth. *Philastrius* labelled
such an interpretation as a downright heresy.

Seventeen Reasons Why "Sons of God" Cannot Be Interpreted as "Sons of Seth"

1. **At no time, before the flood or after, has God destroyed
   or threatened to destroy the human race for the sin of
   "mixed marriages."** It is impossible to reconcile this
   extreme punishment with the mere verbal strictures found
   elsewhere in the Bible for the same practice. If God is
   going to be consistent, He should have destroyed the
   human race many times over!
2. **The contrast made in Genesis 6:2 is not between the
   descendants of Seth and the descendants of Cain, but
   between the "sons of God" and the "daughters of
   men."** If by "sons of God" one means the sons of Seth,
   then only the sons of Seth engaged in mixed marriages--
   what about the daughters of Seth? And only the daughters
   of Cain were involved--what about the sons of Cain?
   Weren't they equally evil in the sight of the Lord?
3. **The strangeness is compounded when we seek for
   evidence that the sons of Seth were godly.** When the

time came for God to destroy the whole human race, he found only one godly family left on the earth--that of Noah. Where were all the other supposedly godly sons of Seth?

Seth's own son could hardly be called righteous. His name was "Enos," meaning "mortal" or "frail" . . . and he certainly lived up to it! Genesis 4:16 is an intriguing verse: *"And to Seth, to him also there was born a son; and he called his name Enos:* **then began men to call upon the name of the Lord.** *"* This statement seems harmless enough, but what does it mean when it says that it was only *then* that men began to call upon the name of the Lord? Upon whom did Adam call? And Abel? And Seth himself? Some scholars give a more literal and more exact translation: *"Then men began to call themselves by the name of Jehovah. "* Others suggest this translation: *"Then men began to call upon their gods (idols) by the name of Jehovah. "* If either is correct, then the evidence for the so-called good line of Seth is non-existent. Enos and his line were as ungodly as the other line. The divine record could not be clearer: *"* **for all flesh** *had corrupted his way upon the earth. "* (Gen. 6:12).

4. **In the Old Testament the designation "sons of God" (bene Elohim) is never once used of humans.** Without exception, the term applies to supernatural beings—beings that are higher than man, lower than God. Only one category of beings fit that designation: *angels.* And the term applies to both good and bad angels. The term is used four times in the Old Testament, each time referring to angels:

■ *Daniel 3:25--"and the form of the fourth is like the Son of God. "* The translation is clearer in modern versions: "like a son of the gods." Since Jesus had not yet become the only begotten Son of God, the reference is to angels.

■ *Job 38:7--*It tells of the "sons of God" shouting for joy when God laid the foundations of the earth. Man had not been created at that time!

■ *Job 1:6 and 2:1* tell of the "sons of God" presenting themselves before the Lord of heaven. Among the "sons of God" is Satan--an angel.

5. **In the New Testament born-again believers are called "sons of God" or "children of God"** (Luke 3:38; John 1:12; Rom. 8:14, etc.) Dr. Bullinger states: *"It is only by the divine specific act of creation that any created being can be called a 'son of God.'"* Thus only three categories of beings qualify for this designation.

■ *Adam*--He was specifically created by God. *"in the likeness of God made he him"* (Gen. 5:1). Adam's descendants were different; they were made in Adam's likeness, and not in God's likeness. Adam *"begat a son in his own likeness, and after his image"* (Gen. 5:3). Adam was a son of God, but his descendants were not.

■ *Angels*--They also were specifically created by God. Lewis Sperry Chafer writes: *"In the Old Testament terminology angels are called sons of God while men are called servants of God. In the New Testament this is reversed. Angels are the servants and Christians are the sons of God."*

■ *Believers*--They are also special and specific creations of God.

6. **In the New Testament, two passages shed light on the subject: Jude 6-7 and 2 Peter 2:4.** These verses make it clear that at some point in time a number of angels fell from their pristine state and proceeded to commit a sexual sin that was both unusual and repugnant.

In Jude 6-7 we find they not only failed to keep their original dominion and authority, but *"left their own habitation,"* a significant word which means "dwelling place" or "heaven." The addition of the Greek word *idion* ("their own") means they left their own private, personal, unique possession. Heaven *was the personal and private residence of the angels. Heaven was never made for man (the earth was for man) but for the angels.* The ultimate destination of the saints will not be heaven but a new and perfect earth (Rev. 21:1-3).

The Greek verb *apoleipo* meant the angels left heaven "once and for all"--aorist tense. It was an irretrievable decision. They crossed the Rubicon. Kenneth Wuest says it was *"apostasy with a vengeance."*

The specific sin they committed is plainly stated. As in Sodom and Gomorrah it was "fornication" and "going after strange flesh." *Strange* (*heteros*) means flesh of a different kind. To commit this sin, the angels had to abandon their own estate and domain and invade a realm that was divinely forbidden to them.

Alford states: *"It was a departure from the appointed course of nature and seeking after that which is unnatural, to other flesh than that appointed by God for the fulfillment of natural desire."*

The mingling of these two distinct orders of beings was contrary to Divine law, and summarily led to God's greatest act of judgment ever enacted upon the human race.

7. **1 Corinthians 11:10**. Paul instructs a woman to cover her head as a sign of subjection to her husband, and also *"because of the angels."* Could this refer back to Genesis 6? Why the sudden reference to angels? Paul believed that an uncovered woman was a temptation to the angels-- without doubt a reference to Genesis 6. William Barclay says: *"There was an old rabbinic tradition which alleged that it was the beauty of women's long hair that attracted the angels of Genesis."*

8. **The offspring of this union** were so extraordinary that it indicates an unusual parentage. In no way could the progenitors of such beings be ordinary humans. The

mother or father could be, but not both.

9. **God's law of reproduction,** according to the biblical account of creation, is *"everything after his kind."* This law makes it impossible for a race of giants to be produced by normal parentage. To produce such monstrosities as the Nephilim pre-supposes supernatural parentage.

10. **Nephilim is a Hebrew word translated in KJV as "giants" (Gen. 6:4).** It is true they were giants in more senses than one, however "Nephilim" does not mean "giants." It comes from the root *naphal* meaning "fallen ones." Most modern versions leave the word "Nephilim" untranslated. The Greek Septuagint translated "Nephilim" as *gegenes.* The word suggests "giants," but actually it has little to do with size or strength. *Gegenes* means "earth born." The same term was used to describe the mythical Titan beings that were partly celestial and partly terrestrial in origin.

Neither the Hebrew nor the Greek word excludes the presence of great physical strength. Indeed, a combined supernatural-natural parentage would imply such a distinctive. Angels are frequently referred to as strong and mighty. No evidence exists anywhere that the offspring of merely mixed marriages would be anything like the Nephilim.

When the word Nephilim is used in Numbers 13:33, the question of size and strength is explicit. We are left in no doubt as to their superhuman prowess. Joshua's spies reported back and said they were like grasshoppers compared with the Nephilim.

Numbers 13 refers to a second eruption of fallen angels, since the earlier Nephilim had been destroyed in the flood. There is an allusion to this in Genesis 6:4, *"There were giants in the earth in those days; and also after that. . . . "* This second eruption explains the severity of God's command to Joshua to exterminate the Canaanites completely. This is the only other instance in the Bible that approximates the flood of Genesis 6.

11. **In Isaiah 26:14 we find there is no resurrection for the Nephilim.** *"They are dead, they shall not live; they are deceased, they shall not rise. . . ."* The Hebrew word for "deceased" is *Rephaim.* It would have saved a lot of misinterpretation if the translators had left the word in the original. *"Dead, they shall not live; Rephaim, they shall not rise."* *Rephaim* is generally understood as one of the branches of the Nephilim. Humans will all be resurrected, but not the Nephilim.

12. **The Septuagint translates "sons of God" (Alexandrian text) as *angelos*.** (Other Greek texts leave the word as is: "sons of God.") This was the text in existence at the time of Christ--but there is no indication that He ever queried or corrected the translation. We assume He concurred that *angelos* was correct.

13. **Jewish fathers**: How do they interpret Genesis 6:4? They are the ones who are the real experts in the field--it is their language, and they are the ones who preserved the documents. No less an authority than W.F. Allbright tells us: *"The Israelites who heard this section (Gen. 6:2) recited, unquestionably thought of intercourse between angels and women."*

    Philo of Alexandria, a deeply religious man, wrote a brief treatise on this very subject entitled "Concerning the Giants." He renders the phrase "sons of God" as "angels of God." And he took the whole passage as historical. The angels failed to resist the lure of physical desire and succumbed to it. He states that the story of the giants is not a myth, but that it is there to teach us that *some men are earth-born, while others are heaven-born, and the highest of all are God-born.*

14. **The early Church fathers** also took this same position. Justin Martyr, Ireneus, Athenagoras, Tertullian, Lactantius,

Eusebius, Ambrose of Milan. . . . In the words of the Ante-Nicene fathers, the angels fell *"into impure love of virgins, and were subjugated by the flesh. . . . Of those lovers of virgins therefore, were begotten those who are called giants."* Again: *". . . the angels transgressed, and were captivated by love of women and begat children."* It is now accepted by almost all scholars that it was the universal opinion of early Christians that "sons of God" or "sons of Elohim" were not human but angelic beings. The Bible does not say "sons of men" and "daughters of men," but "sons of God" and "daughters of men."

15. **Before the fifth century** hardly anyone can be found interpreting "sons of God" as anything other than angels. Even *Josephus*, that colorful and cosmopolitan historian in his monumental volume, *Antiquities of the Jews*, reveals his acquaintance with the account of the fallen angels and the women of earth. He not only knew it, but tells us that the children of that union possessed superhuman strength, and were also known for their extreme wickedness. He says that they resembled the acts of those men the Grecians call giants. He adds that Noah remonstrated with the Nephilim for their villainy.

16. **Perhaps the simplest argument of all is the most convincing.** If the author of Genesis wanted to refer to the "sons of Seth," he would have just said so. If God had intended that meaning, then God would have seen that it was made plain and clear. The verse would have read: "the sons of Seth saw the daughters of Cain that they were beautiful. . . ." But the Bible meant something far more sinister: sexual union between demons from hell and evil women from earth. *Because of the gravity of such a union, and its dire consequences for the human race, God moved in and destroyed the race before it could destroy itself--* all except for one family that had remained uncontaminated.

This sin was of such proportions that God repented

that He had ever made man (Gen. 6:5-6). Note this statement comes immediately after the reference to the Nephilim.

17. **Why was Noah and his family immune?** Genesis 6:9 states that "Noah was a just man." He stood out as an example of righteousness and godliness in a perverse age. Like Enoch before him, Noah also "walked with God." But there is another reason why Noah was spared, one that has escaped practically all commentators.

    Genesis 6:9 says Noah was "perfect in his generation." Moral and spiritual perfection? Hardly. We know what happened after the flood (Gen. 9:20-23). The Hebrew word for "perfect" is *tamiym*, from *taman*. It means "without blemish," as in Exodus 12:5; 29:1, etc. Just as the sacrificial lamb had to be without any physical blemish, so was Noah's "perfection." In its primary meaning it does not refer to any moral or spiritual quality, but to physical purity. Noah was uncontaminated by the alien invaders. One author writes: *"He alone had preserved their pedigree and kept it pure in spite of prevailing corruption brought about by the fallen angels."* Another writes: *"Noah's bloodline had remained free of genetic contamination."*

    This implies that all other families on earth at that time had been contaminated by the Nephilim. It shows that the assault of Satan on the human race had been far more extensive than realized. Is it any wonder that God pronounced such a universal fiat of judgment. The demonic realm attempted to pervert the human world. By genetic control and the production of hybrids, Satan was out to rob God of the people He had made for Himself.

    Even more, if Satan had succeeded, he would have thwarted God's plan for the redemption of the world. He would have hindered the coming of the "seed of the woman," Jesus Christ.

Why then should so may scholars and commentators, including evangelicals, favor ''sons of Seth''? The only argument they produce that carries any validity is that of *rationality*. ''Sons of Seth'' is more palatable to human reason. Reason can never subscribe to the incredible notion that fallen angels could have sexual relations with women of earth. Angels have no physical bodies. Angels do not marry. Angels belong to an entirely different sphere of being. The mind revolts against such absurdity! Settle then for an easy, rational interpretation: sons of Seth, daughters of Cain.

What if every statement in Scripture was interpreted in that way! If it is not reasonable or rational, find another meaning! To impose a human interpretation at the expense of the obvious meaning of the Divine Word is nothing but a *rape of the biblical text*. After all is said, when one deals with the world of the supernatural, rationality is never an argument.

And it was God's own Son, and no one else who said that the major event of the final days will be a repetition of what happened in the days of Noah. His words were these: *''But as the days of Noe were, so shall also the coming of the Son of man be''* (Matt. 24:37). Prophets and preachers have put their emphasis on fires and floods, famines and pestilence, storms and earthquakes, wars and rumors of wars . . . things that have happened dozens, scores, hundreds of times. But Jesus warned us that something happened in the days of Noah that will happen again in the end of time. Noah is the key figure in prophecy.

What happened in his days? Many things, but the outstanding major one was the appearance on earth of beings from space, in order to have unlawful, sexual conduct with women on earth. This event has not characterized any age except that of Noah, and that of our age today. What ruined the ancient world will attempt to ruin our world again. What Jesus said will come to pass. Not only will UFOs arrive, but more importantly, space beings will arrive in them. As in the days of Noah, so in the days of the coming of the Son of man.

Fortunately, we know how the battle will end. We have been given a preview of tomorrow's headlines: "*. . . The kingdoms of this world are become the kingdoms of our Lord, and of his Christ; and he shall reign for ever and ever*" (Rev. 11:15).

Chapter Nine

The Revived Roman Empire
God's Number Two Prophetic
Sign of the Last Days
N.W. Hutchings

According to the thirteenth chapter of Revelation, just prior to the Second Coming of Jesus Christ, one man will have power and authority over all the world. His authority will be three-fold:

> Political Authority: *". . . and power was given him over all kindreds, and tongues, and nations . . . "* (Rev. 13:7).
>
> Ecclesiastical Authority: *"And all that dwell upon the earth shall worship him, whose names are not written in the book of life . . . "* (Rev. 13:8).
>
> Economic Authority: *". . . no man might buy or sell, save he that had the mark, or the name of the beast, or the number of his name"* (Rev. 13:17).

Many scriptures infer that this man will not gain control of the world through military conquest. It is stressed, as we see in Revelation 13:7, "power was given him." Of the nations that comprise the seat of the kingdom of this coming world dictator, we read in Revelation 17:13, *"These have one mind, and shall give their power and strength unto the beast."* Prophetically, this future king of planet earth is called the Beast, the son of perdition, the little horn, the man of sin, the king of fierce countenance, that wicked one, enemy of everything that is God, and in 1 John 2:18 he is referred to as Antichrist.

Jesus said that as it was in the time of Noah, so it would be when He came again. Due to the fact that the antediluvians lived to be hundreds of years old, the population could have reached fifteen billion in the pre-flood world. From the time of Noah, it required forty-five hundred years (A.D. 1850) for the earth's population to reach one billion souls. However, in just the past one hundred and fifty years, world population has increased by five billion. One billion have been born in just the past ten years, and soon one billion will be added each year, then each month, etc. The Church is falling behind in the numbers game. Will hell enlarge itself again, or will a merciful God intervene as He did at the time of the flood? The answer is obvious--God must intervene through the Second Advent of His Son to save the world.

As mankind looks to the problems looming just over the horizon, the nations are clamoring for a world savior. The League of Nations was the first attempt, then the United Nations, and now politicians wishfully consider a New World Order. Along with the political structure, men are devising a world economic system such as the Common Market, NAFTA, the Pacific Rim alliance, etc. Also, the world's ecclesiasticals have been attempting to formulate a world religion. The Islamic religion believes that one day all nations will worship Allah; the World Council of Churches has attempted to bring all churches under one religious shelter; the Roman Catholic Church believes that one day all religions will acknowledge the pope as God's vicar on earth. That a one-world political, economic, and religious system under the authority of Antichrist will be a reality is certain, but the question is how and where will it be focused.

Jeane Kirkpatrick, former U.S. ambassador to the United Nations, stated on December 11, 1991:

"If the Administration has a vision of a New World Order, it is time to share it with Europeans and Americans, because a New World Order is precisely what is emerging on the continent of Europe today."

Jeane Kirkpatrick has been credited by many as being one of the most comprehensive authorities on world politics living today. So why should she predict that the formation of a world government would be centered in Europe?

The consistent view of pre-Millennial exponents of eschatology also has been that a world government which would bring forth Antichrist would be centered in the Revived Roman Empire of Europe. Dr. J.A. Seiss, a noted Christian author of the nineteenth century, wrote in 1860:

"Think for a moment, for there is such a power; a power that is everywhere clamouring for a common code, a common currency, common weights and measures; and which is not likely to be silenced or to stop till it has secured a common centre on its own independent basis, whence to dictate to all countries and to exercise it own peculiar rule on all kings and nations of the earth . . . and which western Europe in its own defence will presently be compelled to construct" (The Apocalypse).

The Parade of Empires

In the second chapter of Daniel the pre-recorded

history of world empires is revealed. According to Daniel's interpretation of King Nebuchadnezzar's dream, there would be four empires that would control the known world until the time that God would set up a kingdom on earth that would never pass away. It is evident from the dispensational plan and purpose of God that this everlasting kingdom will be under the power, rule, and authority of His Son, our Lord Jesus Christ.

In accordance with Daniel's prophecy, Babylon fell to Medo-Persia in 538 B.C.; Medo-Persia fell to Alexander of Greece in 333 B.C.; Alexander died in 320 B.C. and his empire existed in a four-part divided state until about 160 B.C. It was at that time that a new empire rising up in the west began to slowly but surely expand its influence and control throughout the Mediterranean. The only real obstacle to Roman domination was Carthage, and finally in 146 B.C. Rome completely destroyed the city and a new world empire was born. Over the next one hundred years Roman legions moved north to England and Germany, across North Africa, and eastward to India. Unlike Alexander, Rome moved slowly but thoroughly. Roman armies simply refused to accept defeat, as evidenced at the four-year siege of Jerusalem and the two-year siege of Masada.

Roman History

The history of Rome began in about 1000 B.C. Prior to this date, the Italian peninsula was a volcanic region. With the decrease of volcanic activity, the land began to cool and the environment became suitable for habitation. Many peoples from the Mediterranean region settled the land, including the Etruscans, Sabines, and Italians. The Estrucans gained the upper hand and entered into competition with Carthage and Tyre for Mediterranean trade and commerce. In 499 B.C. the other subjugated peoples united and defeated the Estruscans. Because of the multi-national and racial identities of the people who now must replace the rule of the Etruscans, it was agreed to form a democratic type of government patterned after Greece, except it would be more republican than strictly democratic. The single legislative branch was called the Senate. In practice, the U.S. Senate and the British House of Lords subsequently followed the general political pattern. The senators were usually wealthy land owners or commercial barons from the provinces, who served without salaries. It is claimed that there were actually only seventeen paid employees in the government. Of course, foreign governors, tax collectors, and bureaucrats had to live off the fat of the land. In 450 B.C. the various racial and tribal factions agreed on a common Roman legal and judicial system which was embodied in a document called the Twelve Tablets. This mandate or constitution guaranteed all Roman citizens equal justice in court.

The Roman senators usually numbered between six hundred and one thousand. The senators elected or appointed a single governmental leader, called Caesar. ''Kaiser'' is German for Caesar, and ''czar'' is Russian for Caesar. Because of the many religions of nations included within the boundaries of the empire, pantheons were erected where the many gods could be united in one house of worship. A Roman Caesar could be deified as a god, but only after death. The Senate had trouble enough getting along with Caesar without making him a god. In fact, the average reign of a Roman Caesar was only five years and few died of old age. Emperors who reigned more than ten years, like Caesar Augustus at the time of the birth of Jesus Christ, were exceptions rather than the rule. For this reason, most Caesars were adopted sons.

For one thousand years the political fortunes of Rome fluctuated during periods of war and depression. At times it appeared that Rome would fall like the empires before it, but for one thousand years it survived. But like all empires there came a time when the political center of the empire and the moral and patriotic reserve of the people could not support its outreach. In about A.D. 500 Rome, as a world empire, simply disappeared.

The Iron Empire In Prophecy

Rome was represented in the iron legs of the image in Nebuchadnezzar's dream. According to Daniel, there would be only four empires from the time of Babylon until the stone empire that would be established by God. In chronological order, it is obvious that the legs of iron represented Rome. In the replay of the dream of Nebuchadnezzar, Daniel saw the legs on the image breaking into pieces, grinding against each other, and bruising the entire image. While Rome did seemingly disappear in A.D. 500, each of the chunks continued to live as smaller Roman empires. So Rome broke up into many empires--the German Empire, the Italian Empire, the Belgium Empire, the Dutch Empire, the French Empire, the Spanish Empire, the British Empire, etc. Therefore, Rome never actually died. It continued to live and expand in a different form. Of the fourth kingdom, the Roman Empire, we read in Daniel 7:23,

"... *The fourth beast shall be the fourth kingdom upon earth, which shall be diverse from all kingdoms, and shall devour the whole earth, and shall tread it down, and break it in pieces.*"

As prophesied, Rome was indeed different from previous world empires. It tread down the whole earth in a broken form. Every foot of Africa became properties of the European colonial system; at one time the European powers owned every foot of North America. South America was divided between Portugal and Spain, and the sun never set on the British Empire from Sidney to Bombay to Cairo to Baghdad. Even though Rome in its broken state tread down the whole earth, no one could put the pieces together. Charles the Great under the auspices of the Holy Roman Empire could not; the Hapsburgs could not; Napoleon couldn't; Kaiser Wilhelm of Germany couldn't; and neither could Hitler. In fact, Daniel prophesied that toward the end of the age the Roman Empire would be divided even further.

Break Up of Colonial Rome

After World War II, Churchill of England met with Stalin of Russia and Roosevelt of the United States. The meeting was held at Yalta, and Churchill was informed by the other two that the colonial system of Europe had ended, and the colonies must be given up. Churchill protested that England had not fought the war to see the dissolution of the British Empire. However, it happened just as prophesied, because Daniel said that the chunks off the legs must be broken up into many smaller pieces. Jesus had emphasized the budding of the fig tree, meaning the refounding of Israel as a nation as a sign of His return. But Luke quotes Jesus as saying, ''. . . *Behold the fig tree, and all the trees''* (Luke 21:29). After Israel became a nation in 1948, nation after nation from the colonial system was granted independence. The number of nations rose from seventy to one hundred and seventy. But then, Daniel said that ten of the pieces would come together to form a new empire, which would be the revival of the Roman Empire. *''And in the days of these kings shall the God of heaven set up a kingdom, which shall never be destroyed . . .''* (Dan. 2:44).

Back Together Again

Even after the break-up of the Roman Empire, representatives from the nations of Europe met at Versaille, France near Paris to trade and negotiate for raw materials and products not common at all. These annual affairs were called the Common Market. After the European nations lost their colonies after World War II, there was again need for these common markets. Therefore, in 1957 six of the nations together entered into a Common Market alliance at the Vatican under the auspices of the pope. DeGaulle of France, fearing United States entrance into the Common Market, kept other nations from joining until 1972. Since 1972 membership has grown to twelve. Two of the present membership, England and Denmark, have threatened to withdraw—England fearing loss of sovereignty and Denmark fearful of a Catholic majority.

In 1990 speaking at the 339th commencement exercises at Harvard University, German chancellor Helmut Kohl said:

> *"The United States of Europe will thus form the core of a peaceful order in which the nations . . . overcome former rivalry, chauvinist thinking, and mutual prejudice."*

It is to be noted that the United States of Europe is to be the "core" of a world order.

In December 1991 it was announced that the E.E.C. was to be united as one empire under the Maastricht Treaty. In 1992 efforts were entered into to get all twelve nations to confirm the treaty. On December 31, 1992, representatives of all twelve E.E.C. nations met at Edinburgh, Scotland. All the representatives, including Majors of England, Kohl of Germany, and Mitterand of France, expressed confidence in a federal Europe that would shape the world of the future. At the stroke of midnight, one thousand beacons were ignited across Europe. The *London Daily Mail* of January 1, 1993 announced, "1,000 Blazing Beacons Mark Birth of Europe Single Market." But why one thousand beacons? The framers of a new European empire believe Federated Europe will be the light of the world for the next one thousand years.

Although the E.E.C. alliance was purposed only as an economic, cooperative union, at Maastricht in Holland when the new treaty was introduced, it included plans for a powerful political center. An AP news release dated December 12, 1991 stated in part:

> *"To add political muscle to their economic strength, German chancellor Helmut Kohl and French president Francois Mitterand re-*

*vived the decades-old dream of a united Eu-
rope. They sought a transfer of national sovereignty to the community''*

According to Revelation 17 which prophetically refers
to the Revived Roman Empire, the leaders of the alliance
*''. . . have one mind, and shall give their power and strength
unto the beast''* (vs. 13). Already this has happened, with only
Denmark and England expressing doubtful fears, but the
London Daily Express of October 13, 1992 said that DeLors,
leader of the E.E.C., has plans to continue the alliance with
Britain and Denmark.

The September 27, 1992 edition of *The European*
displayed a front-page cartoon showing E.E.C. leaders beside
Humpty Dumpty. Over the cartoon was the headline: "Back
Together Again." When was Europe ever together in the first
place? Only within the boundaries of the old Roman Empire.
Therefore, even the nations within the E.E.C. realize this is
indeed a restoration of the Roman Empire that controlled the
world for almost one thousand year, and the E.E.C. today is
also a revival of that dream. But when this happened, Daniel
said the time for God to set up His own kingdom on earth would
be at the door.

Roman Universal Economic Control

As we have presented, it appears the political structure
for the restoration of the Roman Empire is in place and ready
to be implemented. However, we should remember that Rome
also had economic power over all the known world. We read
in Luke 2:1, *"And it came to pass in those days, that there went
out a decree from Caesar Augustus, that all the world should
be taxed.''* This meant that every individual in the known world
at that time was to be recorded on the Roman tax rolls. This
meant that everyone who worked, bought, or sold, was
financially accountable to Rome. Every item of commerce that

moved was taxed by the Roman tax collectors. Therefore, it should be no surprise that we read of the Antichrist, the ruler of the Revived Roman Empire in Revelation 13:16-17:

> *"And he causeth all, both small and great, rich and poor, free and bond, to receive a mark in their right hand, or in their foreheads: And that no man might buy or sell, save he that had the mark, or the name of the beast, or the number of his name."*

To date, the nearest the world has come to a common economic and financial system has been the World Bank and the International Monetary Fund. The American dollar has served as the nearest thing to a common world currency, but what we see within the Revived Roman Empire is everyone accountable to the Antichrist, just as everyone in the world was accountable to Caesar Augustus. Also, in the Revived Roman Empire everyone, in order to work, buy, or sell, must do so by using marks and numbers. This certainly appears to be a cashless society and an extension of the present computerized coding and marketing system. The E.E.C. has in common usage a common monetary unit, the E.C.U. dollar, worth about twenty percent less than the American dollar. The E.E.C. is counting on the continuing lowering of confidence in the U.S. dollar until the E.C.U. dollar will become the world's common monetary unit. But beyond the E.C.U. we see Europe in the immediate future going to a cashless monetary system. An article in the May 28, 1992 edition of *The Express Line*, a publication of the Oklahoma Publishing Co., described the use of smart cards. These cards are used to purchase anything from shoe strings to automobiles, and this computerized card will also give information on the individual—his age, place of employment, health defects, credit rating, etc. The article from *The Express Line* states in part:

"But even though the number of smart cards have more than doubled since 1988, this country still isn't wise to the cards. Only about one million are in use here compared to one hundred and fourteen million in Europe."

In other words, only about one in three hundred Americans use cashless cards, while in the E.E.C., one in three already use them.

A full page article in the June 24, 1993 edition of the *London Daily Mail* illustrates how shopping in the E.E.C. will be in the future. In fact, the article states that the process is also being tested in some markets. The housewife goes into the supermarket where there are no clerks present. She puts the items she needs in her cart, runs her cart through an automatic scanner, runs her computerized numbered card through the check-slot, then for identification places her hand on a scanner. The article states, *"An alarm would sound if anyone tried to leave with anything that had not been scanned."* The article continues to state that in the future, a home scanner attached to the television could be passed over the food cabinet and any items needed would be delivered to the door. We quote,

"Fiber optics are already being used by phone companies, and technology could be developed for a video phone using the family television."

Of course, without a code mark or a number, no food could be purchased. If this seems far out, remember that *London Daily Mail* is one of the largest newspapers in the world. It is not a religious publication.

In July of 1993 I received from the E.E.C. a copy of the universal coding system used. The program is called INTERSTAT. It consists of seven hundred pages. Within the program, every item in the world sold, purchased, manufactured, or grown, is given a computer number. In order to do business with the E.E.C. the item sold or purchased must have a computer number.

In June 1990 I traveled on Air France and in the airline's monthly magazine, titled *Atlas*, was an article about growing world trade and commerce control by the E.E.C. As of that date, the E.E.C. already had thirty-six percent of the world's currency reserves and forty-four percent of world trade. The commercial power of the E.E.C. is growing through associate memberships, which already number more than thirty. Every employer in the world is receiving an ISO 9000 Fact Sheet. The one I have before me (as I write this article) was posted on the bulletin board of the South Wire Rod and Cable Company of Harvesville, Kentucky. It reads:

"Our world is quickly becoming ISO regulated. What is ISO 9000? It's a European driven series of guidelines for a global quality system. If a company wants to sell products or services in Europe after 1993, it will have to have ISO 9000 certification."

The article continues to explain that with growing E.E.C. commercial influence in the world, that all the world will so become E.E.C. ISO regulated. The president of the E.E.C. is a man by the name of Jacques DeLors. He is a Frenchman. He is a devout Roman Catholic who takes his orders from the Vatican, and he is more anti-American than Charles DeGaulle. The E.E.C. will shut out the United States from European markets, and world markets if possible, by claiming that American products, either manufactured or agriculture, do not meet required world standards.

So what we see in Europe today is a developing commercial system where no cash or checks will be used—all business will be transacted by computer marks and numbers. We also see a commercial system that, when and if it gains dominance, will allow no competition. It is an extension of the old Roman system within the designs of the Revived Roman Empire. If it comes to fruition, then truly no one in the world will be working, buying, and selling without using the E.E.C., the commercial system of Antichrist—marks, and numbers.

Roman Ecclesiastical Control

As we have already noted, besides political and economic control of all nations, the Antichrist will also have absolute ecclesiastical authority: *"And all that dwell upon the earth shall worship him, whose names are not written in the book of life..."* (Rev. 13:8). There is no evidence in Scripture that the Romans forced the Jews to worship Caesar or the pagan gods who were idolized in the Roman pantheons, the main one being in Rome. As the *Encyclopaedia Britannica* notes, no Caesar could be deified until after he died, however there are some historical footnotes that the Romans did try to put the idol of Caesar Augustus in the Temple at Jerusalem. However, the Romans did have a serious problem with Christians. The God whom the Christians worshipped had died, but He was raised again; He would return and judge the world. Eusebius wrote that before Constantine, as many as five thousand Christians a day were crucified, burned, or fed to wild beasts, every single day within the Roman Empire. The Romans were perhaps the most cruel of all people in history in obtaining their goals. Josephus records that at Jerusalem during the siege, the Romans would bring between five hundred and one thousand Jews every day before the walls, beat them until they could not stand, and then crucify them to try to force the Jews inside the city to surrender. At Masada the Romans put Jews in front of their assault machines so that the defenders would have to kill their own people first. Nero was perhaps the most cruel and brutal of all in his persecutions of the Christians.

In A.D. 300 the Emperor Constantine supposedly saw a vision of a cross in the sky which turned him from an inept and timid army field commander into a fearless warrior. Constantine subsequently made Christianity the state religion. The traditional Roman brutality against anyone who opposed it was then incorporated into the Roman state church as a matter of doctrine. Down through the Dark Ages and the Middle Ages, anyone who questioned the absolute authority of the church or the pope were put to death, even those who refused to baptize their babies into the church. *Foxe's Book of Martyrs* and *Martyr's Mirror* document the horror and carnage that reigned under the auspices of the state church. At times, thousands were burned at the stake in one day. Of the harlot religious system that will ultimately cause all the world to worship Antichrist as God, we read in Revelation 17:6, *"And I saw the woman drunken with the blood of the saints, and with the blood of the martyrs of Jesus. . . ."*

The Hapsburgs

In A.D. 800 Pope Leo III crowned Charles the Great of France, also known as Charlemagne, emperor of the Holy Roman Empire. The plan was for the pope to anoint the kings of the nations of Europe and thus revive the Roman Empire under the control of the Vatican. Without the blessings of the pope, no contender could be placed upon a throne. This was known as the "Divine Right of Kings"—having derived his authority from the pope, the king likewise was infallible. This plan worked fairly well, but often family ties and other interests interfered. In A.D. 1000, the Hapsburgs appeared. There was a castle in Switzerland. The male offspring of this family estate were called Counts of Hapsburg. The Hapsburgs formulated a plan whereby they would marry their children into the royal families of Europe. The center of their strength was in Austria. There was a saying, "Let others fight, we of Austria marry."

In other words, the Hapsburgs made love, not war, and as they worked their way into the royal households across Europe their alliance was also called the Holy Roman Empire. They were all devout Catholics who worked with the pope at Rome to reunite the nations that were in the old Roman Empire. World War I began over one of the Hapsburgs counts and a marriage contract that went sour. After World War I, the Hapsburgs were outlawed in Europe; nevertheless, they are returning to power today. Otto Hapsburg is a leader in the E.E.C. parliament, and his son, Karl Hapsburg, is now in Croatia pursuing the goal of a Holy Roman Empire, according to a report in the *London Daily Mail*. With the E.E.C. parliament usurping the authority of elected bureaucrats in the nations of Europe, there is now a strong movement to return all Hapsburgs to the thrones of the nations of Europe. These efforts and sentiments have been widely reported throughout the continent. This is one reason that Denmark is nervous about remaining in the E.E.C. During the Protestant Reformation period, the Danes were almost exterminated by Catholic overlords. If England and Denmark should withdraw, the number of the E.E.C. nations would be reduced to ten and it would have an eighty percent Catholic majority.

Fatima II

The harlot of Revelation is depicted as riding on the back of the Beast, the Antichrist and his empire. Of course, this has always been the position of the state church of Europe since the time of Constantine. But, we read in Revelation 17:16,

> *"And the ten horns which thou sawest upon the beast, these shall hate the whore, and shall make her desolate and naked, and shall eat her flesh, and burn her with fire."*

Recently when Pope John II was in Denver (August

1993) he exhorted the young Catholic youth in attendance to shun abortions, birth control, and sexual sins in all their various forms. Yet, the pope did not address a major problem in his church. The July 30, 1993 edition of *USA Today* brings out that in the United States there are over four hundred cases of child abuse by priests that are costing the church up to one billion dollars. In Europe, the problem is even worse. According to Dr. Malachi Martin, a Catholic insider and advisor to the popes, Pope John Paul II does not intend to attempt a reformation within his church. Rather, according to Dr. Martin, the pope believes as an institution his church is doomed. We read on page 456 of Malachi Martin's latest book that though the Soviet Union is broken up, that communism in a new holy terminology is being taught and propagated by the Catholic Church. He also states on page 464,

> *"John Paul, too, must go on presiding daringly but prudently over the disintegration of his Roman Catholic institutional organization."*

So according to Dr. Malachi Martin, a devoted Vatican insider, the Roman Catholic Church as an institution is doomed, because on the horizon is a universal ecclesiastical system. How is this to come about? According to Dr. Martin's report on the plans of the pope, the pope believes that the spirit of God moves in all religions, including Buddhism, Hinduism, Islam, etc. Martin states on page 285 of his book, *Keys of This Blood*:

> *"There will come a day, John Paul believes, when the heart of Islam—already attuned to the figures of Christ and of Christ's mother, Mary, will receive the illumination it needs."*

The reasoning goes: what Hindu wants to become a

Catholic; what Buddhist want to become a Catholic? However, when the great illumination comes, all religions will accept one man as God's vicar on earth. Of course, he believes that man will be himself or a succeeding pope. As brought out by Dr. Martin and other books and newspaper accounts as well, the great illumination is an expected second Fatima. The first Fatima incident occurred in 1917 when the Lady of Fatima, supposedly Mary, the mother of Jesus, appeared to three children at Fatima, Portugal. The children reported that they were told a great miracle would occur on October 13, 1917, at high noon. Although it had rained for twenty-four hours, according to newspaper estimates seventy-five thousand faithful, believing Catholics gathered in anticipation of the miracle. At exactly noon, the clouds parted, the sun seemingly skipped through the thinning vapors, then plunged toward the earth dripping fire. The crowd began to run, screaming in fear that they would be incinerated. But just as suddenly, the sun stopped its descent and returned to its place in the sky. Whether this event happened as reported, or whether it was simply a matter of mass hysteria, we do not know. However, according to several reliable sources, including Malachi Martin, the pope had a vision about a second Fatima, which would be a great illumination to all mankind. The pope's vision is most interesting in light of the activities of the False Prophet foretold in Revelation 13:13-14:

> *"And he doeth great wonders, so that he maketh fire come down from heaven on the earth in the sight of men, And deceiveth them that dwell on the earth by the means of those miracles which he had power to do in the sight of the beast; saying to them that dwell on the earth, that they should make an image to the beast, which had the wound by a sword, and did live."*

We read in Daniel 11:45 that the Antichrist will plant the tabernacles of his palace on Mount Moriah in Jerusalem. The April 6, 1993 edition of the *Jerusalem Post* carried an architectural design of the building the Vatican hopes to build when it moves to Jerusalem. We read in Daniel 11:37 that the Antichrist will not regard the God of his father, but will honor the God of forces. It may be just a coincidence, but Dr. Malachi Martin has an entire chapter in his latest book, *Keys of This Blood*, titled ''Forces of the New Order,'' describing the geopolitical goals of Pope John Paul II. Pope John Paul II was supposed to go to Jerusalem in 1993 but he did not go because a comprehensive peace treaty was not on the table. He will go when such a treaty is ready. Predictions are that the comprehensive treaty establishing the status of Jerusalem and the Temple Site will be on the table possibly in 1994, and not later than early 1997.

In Revelation 13 it is prophesied that the Beast, or Antichrist, will receive a deadly wound yet live. In Rome, according to the *Encyclopaedia Britannica*, Caesar could not be deified as God until after he died. And what we are looking at here is the revived, or restored Roman Empire. The Antichrist, who will be the Caesar of the Revived Roman Empire, will be wounded and all will think he is dead. He will be anointed by the False Prophet as a god, but then he will live. According to 2 Thessalonians 2, it will be then that he goes to Jerusalem, stops Jewish sacrificial worship, and shows himself by television to all the world as God.

What we see being revealed in Europe today in the revival of the Roman Empire is God's second most important sign today that we are indeed living in the extremity of the age when Jesus Christ could return any day to catch His Church away to heavenly places before the Great Tribulation breaks upon the world.

Conclusion

Exhortations for the End of Time

Mark Hitchcock

No study of Bible prophecy is complete without considering our biblical response. As the year A.D. 2000 appears ominously on the horizon in our world, many are heralding the end of the world like never before. This happened with A.D. 1000, and it is happening with the year A.D. 2000 as well. But this is something that has happened throughout man's history. In 1695 Thomas Beverly, a rector in the Church of England, wrote a book predicting the end of the world in 1697. He wrote a second book in 1698 complaining that the world ended in 1697 but no one noticed. I think that sometimes that's the way people look at things today. They keep hearing about the end of the world and the coming of our Lord; they keep seeing that it is not happening, and a cynicism begins to develop in people. However, that attitude is one of the things that 2 Peter 3 tells us people will have in the last days. There will be scoffers saying, "Where is the sign of His coming?"

We cannot know the time of Christ's return, but the Bible says that we can know the season of it. As we look around at the different signs that are taking place, if the Word of God is to be taken literally, then I think the coming of our Lord, we must say, is imminent. There are signs in nature; signs in society; signs in Christendom, that is, in professing Christianity. The Bible says, "... *in the latter times some shall depart from the faith, giving heed to seducing spirits, and doctrines of devils*" (1 Tim. 4:1). There are signs in world politics: the Revived Roman Empire; the dissolution of the Soviet Union; the PLO-Israeli treaty. Things can change so quickly in our world today. Just a few days before the Berlin Wall fell, no one would have dreamed that it would happen. Just a few days before the Soviet Union fell into dissolution, people would never have believed that such an event would come to pass. A treaty between the PLO and Israel was signed on September 13, 1993, and two days before no one knew anything about it. It was held in top secrecy. Things in our world can happen so quickly now, and come to pass with such speed. These truly seem to be the last days before the coming of our Lord.

As we see this age drawing to a close and all the signs that portend the soon coming of Christ, one important question we must all ask ourselves is: How should we live in view of Christ's coming? No study of Bible prophecy is complete without answering this question. In the Bible, prophecy is always practical. Prophetic passages always contain important, practical exhortations for how we are to live in light of the truth we know. John Nelson Darby said this:

> "*If we study the history of the Church, we shall find it to have declined in spirituality exactly in proportion as this doctrine of the expectation of the Savior's return has been lost sight of. And forgetting this truth, it has become weak and worldly.*"

With this thought in mind, let's consider some of the practical influences the material in this book should have on each of our lives.

■ Prophecy should have a cleansing influ-

ence on sinning hearts. As they see the coming of our Lord, people who are involved in sin should be pure, even as Christ is pure (1 John 3:1-3).

■ **It should have a calming influence on suffering hearts.** We see that in John 14, where Jesus says: *"Let not your heart be troubled: ye believe in God, believe also in me. In my Father's house are many mansions: if it were not so, I would have told you. I go to prepare a place for you. And if I go and prepare a place for you, I will come again, and receive you unto myself; that where I am, there ye may be also"* (vss. 1-3).

■ **It should have a comforting influence on sorrowing hearts.** In 1 Thessalonians 4, Paul tells us of the Rapture. The last statement there is: *"Wherefore comfort one another with these words"* (vs. 18).

■ **Prophecy is also to have a controlling influence on us as we serve the Lord**. After talking about the Rapture in great detail in 1 Corinthians 15:58, Paul says: *"Therefore, my beloved brethren, be ye stedfast, unmoveable, always abounding in the work of the Lord, forasmuch as ye know that your labour is not in vain in the Lord."*

■ **Finally, it should have a caring influence on shepherd's hearts.** In 1 Peter 5, Peter's writing tells the shepherds there, the elders among them, to take care of the flock in a loving way, because when the Chief Shepherd appears they will receive the crown of glory.

The study of Bible prophecy is to have all of these effects upon us. However, I want to center on four great effects that focusing on the soon coming of our Lord should produce in our lives which are outlined in 1 Peter 4:7-11.

> *"But the end of all things is at hand: be ye therefore sober, and watch unto prayer. And above all things have fervent charity among yourselves: for charity shall cover the multitude of sins. Use hospitality one to another without grudging. As every man hath received the gift, even so minister the same one to another, as good stewards of the manifold grace of God. If any man speak, let him speak as the oracles of God; if any man minister, let him do it as of the ability which God giveth: that God in all things may be glorified through Jesus Christ, to whom be praise and dominion for ever and ever. Amen."*

You notice that he begins at the beginning of verse 7 and says, "But the end of all things is at hand." If this was written around A.D. 60, how could someone say that it was at hand? Well, some take "the end of all things" to be the destruction of Jerusalem, but I don't think that is a good interpretation. I think he is looking far beyond that event. Others say that it is the Rapture of the Church. Some say "the end of all things" is the Second Coming of Christ. Others take it as the destruction of everything we know, that is, the heavens and the earth, and the new heavens and the new earth are being prepared. I don't know that one can be real dogmatic about which of those last three that is, but for us, as believers, "the end of all things" in this life is when the Rapture of the Church takes place. I think the best application for us is when our Lord comes and receives us to Himself. Peter says, "the end of all things is at hand,'' or it is near. It has always been true, ever since the first century Church, that the coming of our Lord ''is at hand.''

Of course, one of the reasons is that to God a day is as a thousand years, and a thousand years is as a day. In His sight it is simply fleeting moments of time. So every generation in history can look at the Word of God and see things that are happening, and say that the coming of our Lord indeed is at hand. But you notice what he says next: ''But the end of all things is at hand . . . therefore. . . .'' Now, what Peter does is that he tells them that if the end of all things is really at hand, here is how you are to live your life in view of the coming of our Lord. Peter tells them four main things.

Keep Your Head Clear

The first thing he tells them in the last part of verse 7 is to keep their head clear during this time. He says, ''be of sound judgment, and sober spirit for the purpose of prayer.'' The words ''sound judgment'' is an imperative. It is something they are commanded to do, It means that they are to be serious. It means they are to think in a level-headed or clear way. You and I are not to get caught up in some type of a prophetic frenzy. We are not to get so excited about Christ's coming that we fail to live out our present responsibilities. This was a common problem in the early Church. They expected our Lord's coming so imminently that sometimes some of them would quit working--just like some people do today who go out and get in their pajamas on the mountain top and wait for Him to come. But Peter says, ''If you see the coming of our Lord drawing near, be of sound judgment. Don't get caught up in some type of prophetic frenzy. Don't get off balance.''

We see a lot of this today. People make statements such as, ''Gorbachev is the Antichrist; this person is the Antichrist; this is going to happen.'' People get caught up in a frenzy of prophetic material, and they get so excited that they get off balance.

The *Wall Street Journal* carried an article a couple of years ago entitled, "Millennium Fever; Prophets Proliferate; The End Is Near." The subheading read: "As the year 2000 approaches Guru Ma, among others, says 'head for the hills.'" It describes one man and says:

> *"Louis Defoe, a former vice-president of Chase Manhattan Bank, packed up his family and his own investment banking business last July and moved to Montana. And not just to get away from New Jersey. He wanted to escape the earthquakes, economic collapse, and nuclear war his religious sect anticipates in the 1990s. Mr. Defoe bought twenty acres of sagebrush with a mountain view in Paradise Valley. He also gathered a five-year supply of canned squash, carrots, and broccoli, a stack of treasury bills, several tens of thousands of dollars in gold coins, and a five-bed apartment in a concrete reinforced underground bomb shelter. Though one might wonder what use a T-bill would be in an atomic attack, Mr. Defoe is serene. He is an adherent of Elizabeth Claire Prophet, the leader of the Church Universal and Triumphant, whose headquarters is nearby, and he believes in being prepared for the worst, because when you're prepared for the worst you have peace of mind."*

I heard a man on the radio recently heralding the end of the world. I didn't really get in on the first of the broadcast to see what his certain angle on this is, but you can send money to him and he'll send you all this information about the survival kit that you need to have. As the year 2000 comes upon us, we are going to hear more and more things like this. You and I need to live every day as if our Lord could come back, *but* we are not to get caught up in a prophetic frenzy of things and get off balance as we do that. We are to be of sound judgment.

He also says we are to be of sober spirit. It means to be clear-headed. Literally what it means is, "don't be drunk." It is the opposite of being intoxicated. It means to have a clear, alert mind. It means to not have fuzzy-type thinking. You and I are to be mentally alert, and see life correctly in view of the coming of our Lord. Peter says we are to do this for the purpose of prayer. All of this should lead us to a life of prayer.

Remember that Jesus told His disciples several times in His last days with them, "Watch and pray." If we are watchful and we see the coming of our Lord, it should lead to prayer in our lives. Colossians 4:2 says: "*Continue in prayer, and watch in the same with thanksgiving.*"

What kinds of things should we be praying about as we see the end of time, as we see Christ's coming on the horizon? One of the things we should be doing is praying for people we know who do not have a relationship with Jesus Christ. We should be on the alert for people who have come into our contact who do not have a relationship with our Lord--those, who if He were to come, would be left behind. And also pray for ourselves that we will have an intensity and a passion about our lives; to live life in view of the coming of our Lord. You know, if we really believed the truth of the imminent coming of Christ, it would radically change the life that every one of us lives. But, it is something we do not think about; it is off down the road somewhere. Oh, of course, we think, "Yeah, it may happen sometime." We think, "Well, those people back in World War II got all caught up in this. Mussolini was the Antichrist; Europe was rising; it looked like everything was coming to pass, but it didn't happen back then, so I am sure this is just another false alarm."

You and I are to live every day as if Christ could return,

and that is to spur us on to prayer. One of my prayers for myself individually is that I will be focused on the things that God would have me be focused upon, the things that the early Church focused on: Jesus Christ crucified, risen, and coming again. That was their focus as a group of people, and that is my prayer for myself, that I won't get off on tangents and different things that cause problems, but that I will focus on the things that are the most important. I think if all of us pray in that way and stay alert, we will be believers who will please our Lord in these last days.

The first thing we are to do in times like these is to keep our head clear; be of sound judgment; be of sober spirit; giving ourselves to prayer. In 1 Samuel 12:23 we read that failing to pray is a sin. Many of us think about a lot of things that we do that are terrible sins that God hates, but there are also sins of omission, and failing to pray is a sin. It is a failure of availing ourselves of the great privilege and a relationship that we have with our God.

Keep Your Heart Warm

The next thing that Peter tells us that we are to do in days like these is to keep our heart warm. He says in verse 8: "And above all things have fervent charity among yourselves: for charity shall cover the multitude of sins." What he literally means where he says, "above all" is "before all things." Before everything else, keep fervent in your love for one another. As I am sure most of you know, the badge of Christianity is our love for one another. In John 13:34-35 Jesus says:

> "A new commandment I give unto you, That ye love one another; as I have loved you, that ye also love one another. By this shall all men know that ye are my disciples, if ye have love one to another."

Colossians 3:14 says:

> *"And above all these things put on charity,*
> *which is the bond of perfectness."*

1 Peter 1:22 says this:

> *"Seeing ye have purified your souls in obeying*
> *the truth through the Spirit unto unfeigned love*
> *of the brethren, see that ye love one another*
> *with a pure heart fervently."*

This is not just something that we are to just give lip service to. It is to come from deep within us--from the heart. This passage says to keep fervent in your love. This word "fervent" means "deeply." It has the idea of being "strained" or "stretched." It was used of a horse being at full gallop when its muscles are stretched to the limit. In other words, what he is saying is that our love is to be stretched out; that is, true love will stretch but it will never reach a breaking point. That is the love you and I are to have for one another, especially when we see that the end of all things is at hand--the kind of love we are to have in our families, the love we are to have in our churches, the love we are to have for others who are outside the body of Christ. We are called in days like these to keep our hearts warm. The statement in this verse is in the present tense, which means to keep giving yourselves to it; keep fervent in your love continuously for one another as you see that the coming of our Lord is at hand.

The last part of this verse says, "for charity shall cover the multitude of sins." This is a beautiful statement. It has been taken by some to mean that love covers our own sins, or that God's love covers our sins. However, the best way to understand it is that love will forgive and overlook the faults and failures in other people. One of the great things that we need today is to cover the sins of other people. Now, it doesn't mean to condone other people's sins. Or, obviously, if someone has committed an egregious sin, that is, if we know someone has done something against the law, we obviously are not going to cover that up. However, we are to cover the faults and the failures that each of us have, rather than broadcasting those failures and stirring them up. That is what love will do. Proverbs 10:12 says, *"Hatred stirreth up strifes: but love covereth all sins."* 1 Corinthians 13:7 says that love *"beareth all things."*

If you really love someone you are not going to go out and broadcast their faults to everybody else. This is one of the things that I think is most damaging in a family relationship, or between a husband and wife, that is, when people don't cover one another's liabilities and shortcomings. Those of you who are married know how much you appreciate it when your spouse doesn't broadcast all of your faults and failures and shortcomings to everyone else. Really loving somebody means you are going to cover their faults and failures. You are going to forgive them and not broadcast those to other people.

Mark Twain had a terrible habit of swearing, and it was very upsetting to his wife. She tried her very best to cure him of it. One day when he was shaving he cut himself, and he recited his entire vocabulary of words. When he was finished, his wife, hoping to shock him, repeated every word that he had just said. Twain was stunned by her saying and said calmly, "You have the words, dear, but you don't know the tune."

Throwing our faults and our failures up to one another is something that we should not do when we see the coming of our Lord at hand. A friend who knew George Bernard Shaw and his wife said that she noticed that all the time he was speaking, his wife was always knitting. The friend asked her, "What are you knitting?" Mrs. Shaw said, "Oh, nothing in particular. It's just that I've heard these stories of his a thousand times, and if I don't do something with my hands I'd choke him." We all recognize that there are faults and failures in the people that we know that bother us, but our responsibility as the end of all things is at hand, is to cover a multitude of sins in one another. We need to do this in our churches as well. When we know failures and faults that other people have, we are to go and talk with them about it. Seek them out and make things right, but do not broadcast it to other people. Be ready to forgive; willing to forgive; and love one another.

Keep Your Home Open

The next thing that Peter tells us to do, in verse 9, is to keep our home open. He says, ''Use hospitality one to another without grudging.'' Back in that day there were not very many motels or inns, and those that were available were very uncomfortable and very expensive. Therefore, it was necessary for travelers to stay with other people. It was very important for believers to be hospitable to one another. What Peter is telling us is not only to be hospitable, which means to be a lover of strangers, but to do it without complaint. Now, anybody can help people out, but it is another thing to do it without complaint. There are six times in the New Testament, at least, that we are told specifically to be hospitable to one another. Romans 12:13 tells us to be practicing hospitality. In 1 Timothy 3 and Titus 1 this is a qualification for those who would be elders. They are to be lovers of strangers, those who practice hospitality. The idea here is to have generosity without grumbling--to love those who are strangers.

Lack of hospitality is a glaring failure in the lives of many believers. There can be kind of a coldness, or a cliquish environment in the local church. However, in view of the fact that the end of all things is at hand, we are called upon to continuously practice hospitality, to be lovers of strangers. We all know that when we come into a new group of people, there is nothing more encouraging to us than to have someone reach out to us and talk with us, encourage our heart, and to have us over into their home for fellowship with them. That is something that all of us deeply enjoy and desire, but it is something in our day and time that it seems we are too busy to practice. Everyone is running their kids to baseball, or to the ballet, to this or that. Everyone is caught up in such a frenzy of activity all the time, that we fail to practice true Christian hospitality.

I am so thankful that my wife is one who is given to hospitality. We sit down and try to plan out having people over, and we make it a policy to get together with strangers. It is easy to have your best friends over all the time; that is comfortable, easy. But to have people over that we do not know is difficult and challenging. I have been amazed at several of the things that have happened just in our neighborhood. My wife and another lady who attends my church have ministered to the people and barriers have broken down. There is no amount of preaching or sharing with people, or anything else that can replace simple hospitality to strangers and showing them how much we care. I don't think there is anything that will go as far as that in our Christian testimony.

But you notice what says in 1 Peter 4:9 : "do it without grudging." One of the reasons I think so many times that we do not practice hospitality is because we are afraid they might come over to our house and stay late, or their kids might mess up the house, or we might get some dirt on the floor, or that we are going to have to go out of our way a little bit. Then when people leave there is complaining about it. But Peter says not only should we show hospitality, but we are not to complain about it. Do it with joy. Have people over to your home, open it up to them, and do it without complaint. There is so much in us that is selfish. We are so selfish with our things and keeping them just they way they are. That is one of the main preventions to us being hospitable to one another. Christ is calling on us as the end of all things is at hand to reach out to people around us that we do not know, and show true Christian hospitality to them, without complaint.

Keep Your Hands Busy

The next thing Peter tells us in verses 10 and 11 where I want to focus the rest of this chapter is to "keep your hands busy." Not only are we to keep our head clear, our heart warm, and our home open, but we are to have our hands busy about the business of our Lord. There are four main passages in the New Testament that deal with the subject of spiritual gifts: 1 Corinthians 12; Romans 12; Ephesians 4; and 1 Peter 4. This passage in 1 Peter is the last one written of all of those on the list. It is also basic. As we will see, it divides all gifts into two main categories. What Peter is telling us here is, as you see that the end of all things are at hand, that the coming of our Lord is near, you need to know what your spiritual gift is and to be practicing it. You need to be busy for our Lord until He comes. I have divided verses 10 and 11 into nine separate parts which I want to look at in these verses.

The first part of this verse is what I would call something that is personal. He says, "as every man." Every believer in Jesus Christ has one or more spiritual gifts—a supernatural Divine enablement and empowerment that God has given that person to serve the body of Christ. 1 Corinthians 12:7 states that to each one is given the "manifestation of the Spirit for the common good." Every person has been given a manifestation of the Spirit for the common good of the body of Christ. I know that many places have questionnaires and surveys you can take to determine your gift. But the first thing we need to understand is that every believer has one. Every believer received a gift, or gifts, at the moment of their conversion.

That brings us to the next part of this verse which says, "hath received." Notice it is past tense. There are many today who are saying we should be seeking a gift, and I think this passage, as well as others, tells us that you already have it. Whatever the gift you have been given, you have already received it. He says, "Each one hath received." It is past tense. Now, there are a couple of places in the book of 1 Corinthians where it says to earnestly seek certain gifts. But if you read those passages, it is in the plural. So I don't take it that an individual should seek to have a certain gift, but that members of a church should seek that certain gifts be manifested among them. It is a seeking corporately that those gifts be in operation in a church. But I do not believe that the Scripture tells an individual believer to seek a certain gift. I think the believer already has that gift, or gifts, and it is incumbent on each believer to discover what it is, and to begin to use it.

The next thing mentioned in this verse is simply the words, "the gift," as each one has received "the gift." The word here is a *charisma*. Every person has a *charisma*--a supernatural enablement by God to do something in a way that other people are unable to do it. You take ten different men with the gift of teaching, and every one of them have that gift in a different way; it goes through their own personality. We need different people with the gift of teaching. One person may be good at a certain line of things; one person may focus on another area. In all the different areas of gifting, it is a Divine enablement that God has given, a manifestation of the grace of God by which the Spirit's effect is manifested in the life of that person. Every believer has received a gift, a *charisma*, for the ministry of the body of Christ.

The next thing that is stated here is "even so, minister the same to one another." Literally, it means to "each other, serving it," and it has the idea of continuously doing this. We are to continuously be serving our gift up to other people. If everyone came to church with the attitude "that when I go to church today I am going to serve up my gift to the other people who are there," the Church would be revolutionized. If we came with that attitude, not of coming to church to be the diner, that is, to be the one to sit down and be waited upon, but to be the waiter, to wait on other people and serve our gifts up to them, what a difference it would make--if we all came to serve, and not to be served. We should all ask ourselves, "What has

God divinely enabled me to do that no one else in my church can do?'' Then we should go to church with the attitude that we are going to serve that gift up to the other people, and to minister to them. This is God's calling to us as the end of all things is at hand.

The next important part of this verse is, ''as good stewards.'' A steward was one in that day who did not have any possessions of his own, but he had been entrusted with those possessions by his master. You and I, in and of ourselves, the Bible tells us, have nothing. However, we have been given a God-given gift and empowerment, and as good stewards we are to use that gift, because some day we will give an account. God has equipped us, He has given us a gift, and that is a stewardship that we have, and we must answer for how we are using that gift that He has given to each of us. There is responsibility and there is accountability for a steward as to how they use what God has given them.

The next thing in this verse he says is, ''of the manifold grace of God.'' This is a beautiful statement in this passage. It means the variegated or multicolored grace of God. Every group of believers is like a picture that is being painted with a little color over here, some more color over there, making a beautiful picture where all the color is in just the right amount, and is all in just the right place. We are good stewards of the multicolored grace of God that He has placed in the body of Christ, manifest in all these different ways.

Next we come to verse 11 and we get the pattern for gifts: ''*If any man speak, let him speak as the oracles of God; if any man minister, let him do it as of the ability which God giveth.* . . .'' There are two basic kinds of gifts that are given in this passage. This is a very helpful passage because it reveals to us that every believer either has a speaking gift or a serving gift, in broad categories. Therefore, once you find out you have a speaking gift or a serving gift, then you can begin to break it down as to what more specific area God has gifted you in. But every believer is gifted either to speak or to serve. Now that does not mean that those who are gifted to serve should never speak, or that those who are gifted to speak should never serve. Never say, "Well, I am just gifted to speak and I don't have to do anything else. I don't have to help people, or care about people, or show mercy." No, we should do all of these things, but there is a Divine enablement that God has given us, either primarily to be one who speaks, or to be one who serves. Speaking would include all forms of oral service that God has in the body of Christ, and service would include all of the service gifts that are listed. Concerning speaking, Peter says, whoever speaks let him speak as it were "the oracles of God." These words, "the oracles of God" in other places always mean "the Word of God." When someone speaks, they are to speak the Word of God. They are not to get up and give their own speculation, or their own philosophy, or their own ideas, but they are to give God's Word. Peter says, "If anyone speaks, he is to speak as it were the oracles of God." He is to speak God's Word. So many things today are made up from Scripture, and it is not speaking as an oracle of God.

There is more to speaking as an oracle of God than just speaking according to the Bible. It means to speak that which is good for that particular moment, for that group of people. The one who is speaking must be sensitive to the Spirit of God. He must speak the message that the people need to hear at that time. Anyone who speaks must speak as an oracle of God. He must speak God's Word and speak the Word that is needed for that moment.

Also, those who serve are to do it by the strength which God supplies. The power for service is supplied by God. The reason so many people get burned out in ministry is because they do it in their own power. Much of what we do in the Christian cause is done in the power of the flesh. The reason I can say that is because I am an expert at it. We all are. We are all experts at doing things in our own strength. We become tired, weary, and burned-out because we are relying on our own power. But God says here in His Word that He is the one who supplies the strength that we need. The word that is used here is the word from which we get ''choreographer.'' Think of a choreographer as the one who designs or creates a dance that people are doing. But in that day the choreographer was the one--not who designed the act--but who funded the act. He was the one who paid for it. He was the one who paid for the chorus or the act, and everything that went into that. In that day if you paid for an act, you had to be very wealthy, because it was something that you had to spend money on lavishly. It means literally to pay the expense of training a chorus for the Greek theater, or to defray the cost or the expense of something. It has the idea of lavishly supplying, and God says that if we speak, or if we serve, we are to do it by the strength which He Himself supplies. If we are involved in God's service there is a price to pay. There is an emotional price to pay to be involved in God's service; there is a physical price to pay; oftentimes there is a material price to pay. But God is saying that He will supply lavishly every need that we have if we will simply do what He has called us to do, and do it in His power. Think of God's grace and His power for us when you are tired and weary in God's service. I know some of you have parents you are caring for; children you are caring for. You are ministering in your church. When you are tired God would simply say, ''Let down your buckets'' into the ocean of His power; there is an abundant supply there available of God's power and His strength. What we do so often is just grit our teeth and say, ''I'll just try a little harder. Maybe I can make it through the day on my own.'' We are just exhausted at the end of the day, because everything we have done has been in the power of the flesh. God is the one who will pay the expenses for our act if we are good stewards with the gifts He has given us and depend on Him.

The final thing he tells us in this verse is the purpose of it all, which is so that in all things God may be glorified through

Jesus Christ, to whom belongs the praise and dominion forever and ever. Amen. Everything we do is to be done for the glory of God. This is the proper end of all Christian service; to do it for the glory of God. This is the most difficult thing for us to do as humans because we want some glory for ourselves.

There is always that one percent, or that five percent there in the back of our mind that seeks glory from other people. God says in Isaiah 41, "My glory to another I will not give." God will not share one percent of His glory with another person. Everything that is to be done is to be done so that in all things He may be glorified. "The chief end of man is to glorify God, and to enjoy Him forever." And the word "Amen" at the end of this verse means, "So it is."

Warren Wiersbe gives the following illustration:

> *"Early in my ministry I gave a message on prophecy that sought to explain everything. I have since filed away that outline and will probably never look at it except when I need to be humbled. A pastor friend who suffered through my message said to me after the service, 'Brother, you must be on the planning committee for the return of Christ.' I got his point, but he made it even more pertinent when he said quietly, 'I've moved from the planning committee to the welcoming committee.'"*

It is important for us to know the signs of the times. But you and I are not on the planning committee for the return of Christ. We do not know for certain when it will occur, but we are to always live as if the end of all things is at hand, and get on the welcoming committee. We are to do the things that this passage tells us to do in view of the coming of our Lord. We are to keep our head clear in days like these; we are to keep our heart warm; we are to keep our home open; and we are to keep our hands busy working for our Lord until He comes. If we do these things that are mentioned in this passage, when our Lord comes He will find us doing His business, and He will be pleased. Then we can hear from Him those precious words, *"Well done, thou good and faithful servant."*